TO BE ONE

A Note from the Publisher

RACISM is one of the major obstacles to world peace. The dignity of human beings is continually undermined by its persistence and the potential of whole groups of people is denied under its tyranny. Any effort to overcome this scourge must be applauded.

Nathan Rutstein's personal story highlights the depth of the problem, one which has even reached into the language itself. The terms used to describe people of color have often been derogatory and imposed by others. It has been some three decades since the black people of North America began to describe themselves as 'Blacks'. In recognition of this as a proper name, in the same sense as Caucasian, we have capitalized the noun 'Black' wherever it appears in this book.

To Be One

A Battle against Racism

by

Nathan Rutstein

GEORGE RONALD
OXFORD

GEORGE RONALD, Publisher
46 High Street, Kidlington, Oxford, OX5 2DN
© NATHAN RUTSTEIN 1988
All Rights Reserved

British Library Cataloguing in Publication Data

Rutstein, Nathan
    To be one. — (Global transformation
    series).
    1. Racism
    I. Title II. Series
    305.8

ISBN 0–85398–278–3

TO WRITE this book I needed hard, honest feedback, and I received it from Roy Jones, Helen Sousa, Daniel Rae, Carol Rutstein, Duane Dumbleton, Karen Streets-Anderson, Richard W. Thomas, Tod Rutstein, Theodies Washington and Paul Robbins.

'Frederick Douglass' is reprinted from *Robert Hayden: Collected Poems*, edited by Frederick Glaysher, by permission of Liveright Publishing Corporation. Copyright © 1985 by Erma Hayden.

The passage on page 128 is reprinted from *To Move the World: Louis G. Gregory and the Advancement of Racial Unity in America* by Gayle Morrison, by permission of the Bahá'í Publishing Trust, Wilmette, Illinois. Copyright © 1982 by Gayle Morrison.

Phototypeset in Great Britain
by Photoprint, Torquay, Devon.
Printed and bound in Great Britain
by Billing & Sons Ltd, Worcester.

Preface

ALTHOUGH I have always been concerned about racism in America, I never thought I would write a book about the problem. I did not feel qualified to do so. It was a friend's challenge that inspired me to write this book.

About a year ago, while writing a text on global transformation, I found myself struggling with a short chapter on racism and I wanted someone whose life experience I respected to read over what I had written. Leonard Smith felt that what I was trying to communicate would have greater value if I drew from personal experience, if I took the 'first person' approach.

Frankly, his suggestion startled me and I went back to my work unconvinced. I do not like writing about myself. However, I could not dismiss Leonard's advice altogether. I was curious to see what would happen if I began to write in the first person. I could always change the approach later if I felt uncomfortable with it, I reasoned.

As I began to write I sensed my feelings and thoughts flowing freely onto the paper. For me, it was an unlocking of the heart. I relived my past involvement and relationships with Blacks. The more I wrote, the greater was the flow of feelings. It was more than a cathartic experience: I was becoming acquainted with the truth. I realized that my racism was a disease, a disease of the heart and mind that still grips America.

After the second chapter I was convinced that I had to complete my story. With every chapter I grew more confident that this approach was the right one. I felt compelled to discuss openly my personal insights. Mine was a genuine desire to describe how one individual coped with the disease and what he did to try to overcome it.

I know there are sections of this book which will be challenged by people who have different interpretations and perceptions of the present racial situation in North America. So be it. I do not claim to be an authority on race relations. I am not a sociologist. One thing, however, is certain: my observations and opinions are based on real life experiences, experiences which reflect our society today.

My hope is that by relating my story those who are similarly afflicted with the disease of racism will be encouraged to seek, with earnest, a cure.

Nathan Rutstein
Amherst, Massachusetts
May 1988

Foreword

Though Nat Rutstein and I come from different backgrounds – he from a Jewish and I from a black Baptist – we share a tradition of struggle for social justice and a religious fellowship. We were both shaped by the social transformation of the 1960s and, more importantly, both of us are members of the American Bahá'í community.

This community was assigned the task by 'Abdu'l-Bahá, the son of the founder of the Bahá'í Faith, Bahá'u'lláh, of creating love and unity between black and white Americans. As a result of this interracial bond, Bahá'ís would contribute to the establishment of world peace. Both black and white Bahá'ís were given the responsibility of helping to solve the problem of racism in America.

Nat has taken on the challenge of writing a book which is basically for whites. While non-whites can read it with profit, it speaks more directly to the racial fears and anxieties of those whites who, while committed to racial equality as an ideal, hesitate to embody the ideal in their personal lives. It encourages them to start the process of transformation within their own hearts and souls, their families and communities.

Nat does not promise easy victories for whites who undertake this process. It is hard work to look inside one's soul, to see the crippling forces of racism and to resolve to spend the rest of one's life eradicating it both in oneself and in society. Nat discovered ugly ghosts hiding in his own psyche. He had to struggle with the hypocrisy which marks many a white liberal's good intentions. He had to give up the false pride so common in white liberals who view themselves as martyrs in the struggle for social justice. He had to acknowledge that the struggle against racism is not over when liberal whites grow weary and decide it is time to return home to mow the lawn and take the kids to piano lessons. The struggle continues until the spiritual transformation of both Blacks and whites is complete and society is healed of the sickness of racism.

Nat's revelations of his racial attitudes at various stages of his transformation can be insulting to black readers and an embarrassment to whites, but he is being painfully honest about a process of becoming – a process which is all too rare within interracial movements. This book should not be read and put back on the shelf. It should be studied by Blacks and whites and acted upon. It should form the basis for a more open and healing dialogue on race relations for all who truly desire to see an interracial world based on social justice, love and unity.

Richard W. Thomas
Associate Professor, History and Urban Affairs
Michigan State University, 1988

1

DISCOVERING truth doesn't always make us happy. It can be a painful experience. It can disturb a way of life that we have grown comfortable with. It can shatter an illusion that we had always accepted as reality. I know what it's like.

As long as I can remember, even as a child, I supported the cause of the oppressed; it didn't matter who they were or where they lived. Every social injustice I witnessed angered me. In time I became sympathetic with those causes that advocated swift changes, even if violence was called for. I was a staunch liberal, and proud of it, willing to take on any reactionary or conservative in an argument and, if need be, a fight.

I had always believed in the oneness of mankind. Many of my friends and relatives felt I was a 'hopeless idealist'. Our arguments led to an uneasy truce. Whenever we gathered we rarely strayed from safe subjects like food, the weather and favorite vacation spots. I could never subscribe to their belief that the human being is simply an animal prone to violence and that humanity isn't meant to be united. Some of my friends who felt that way were extremely religious. Hypocrites, I thought. I wanted nothing to do with religion.

I would have gravitated towards those who shared my views, but there weren't any. In college I refused to become involved with fraternities because of their racist membership policies. In fact, I did my part in trying to eliminate those policies. I went out of my way to befriend the few Blacks on campus, who were socially ostracized. My association with Blacks gave most whites the impression that I was a radical, a malcontent. Deep down I enjoyed being viewed in that light.

I could be myself and not have to play the superficial, often hypocritical, games that were expected of everyone by the campus leaders. I chose to be a rebel because I didn't want to be part of a charade. No one had to convince me that the existing institutions were corrupt. In my heart I knew that a complete transformation of the prevailing order was necessary before there could be true justice. The search for a cause that possessed the power to achieve true justice became an obsession. During my search I discovered something I hadn't expected: my own racism.

Oh, I wasn't a bigot, someone who flaunts his racism. God, no! After all, I had spent a lot of time fighting for human rights causes and, being Jewish, I had been the target of anti-Semitism. Also, some of my friends were black. And I despised the Ku Klux Klan and anything smacking of fascism. I supported every effort to bring about racial equality. My concern for the plight of America's Blacks was so deep that any news of their progress moved me. I cried when I learned that Jackie Robinson had broken the racial barrier in major league baseball. Every time he hit a home-run or made an outstanding field play a sense of pride welled up within me. I wanted to spring from my chair and call all of my black friends and tell them what had just happened. Nevertheless, I was infected with racism.

It took some time to recognize the symptoms. I had a knack of quickly submerging all unpleasant thoughts into the deepest recesses of my mind: a survival technique that became apparent to me only after I realized that I was infected. It was then that I could recall the early signs. One in particular stands out: while I never called anyone a nigger, there were times when I wanted to, the urge usually coming when I was in a stressful situation.

One day I was driving to an important appointment. I didn't want to be late. The black driver in front of me was poking along at 40 miles an hour in a 55 mile an hour zone. I pressed the horn, and the thought 'Move, nigger' flashed through my mind. Though a single incident, quickly forgotten, it was a sign of a more general repressed condition. In time it would surface as evidence of my painful discovery – but not right away. There wasn't the will to diagnose that sick thought which came to me at that stressful moment. I buried it in my subconscious as fast as it darted into my mind. It was to take a traumatic experience to make me clearly recognize the hidden disease of racism within me and begin to ponder seriously how it originated.

That experience materialized like a time-bomb reaching its explosion point. When it happened, I was rendered spiritless, even speechless for a while, my self-esteem terribly damaged. I began to question whether I was worthy of possessing the values I cherished, values I thought had set me apart from racists and those with parochial views. I felt hypocritical, a characteristic I had always found so contemptible in others. At the time the pain was too intense for me to appreciate what I was going to gain from the experience. I wanted to hide; I was unable to think of even the possibility of recovery.

The experience was related to my involvement with the Bahá'í Faith. Shortly before graduation day, Bill, a close college friend who was a Bahá'í, asked me to spend the summer in Chicago, his hometown. He had already introduced me to his religion, whose social teachings I found extremely attractive. But I had other plans: pursuing a law degree in New York was one, and re-acquainting myself with old high school friends and family was another. Frankly, I was looking forward to being in a part of the country that was more progressive socially and politically than the Midwest. Besides, I thought spending a summer in Chicago would be like being in a perpetual sauna. In 1953 air conditioning wasn't as common as it is today.

After only two weeks in New York something strange happened. I had a strong urge to go to Chicago. Friends and family presented sound reasons why I shouldn't leave. But I went anyway, not knowing where I would stay or where I would work.

I was stunned that my college friend expressed no surprise when he found that I was in Chicago. In fact, Bill informed me that he had already arranged for a place for me to live. Spooky, I thought, since I hadn't told him I was coming. When he asked if I minded sharing the apartment with someone else, I told him that I actually felt it was a good idea, since we could split rent and food costs. Bill said that though he'd only known Pete Baker a few weeks, he found him to be an honorable person. Bill's word was good enough for me.

I was delighted with the apartment location. Chicago's near North Side borders on Lake Michigan, and its famous eating places and jazz clubs make it the most cosmopolitan section of the city. And subway transportation was only a block away. The three-room apartment was sunny and fully furnished and even had a large fish tank that glowed at night.

When I learned that my prospective roommate was studying the Bahá'í Faith I was impressed because I was attracted to the religion's liberal teachings. However I had a major stumbling block over anything that smacked of organized religion. The concept of God perplexed me. But, I thought, perhaps this new roommate and I can explore this problem together.

Pete didn't have that problem. But my first meeting with him created a different problem: when Bill introduced me to Pete, I didn't know what to say or do, for I hadn't expected him to be a Black.

I had never thought of having a black roommate, particularly someone so dark. It didn't matter that Pete was a gentle, sweet-natured person who was well read and a former boxing champion. The prospect of living with him frightened me. My latent racism surfaced and for the first time in my life I was unable to shove it back. At that moment I wasn't thinking about how those feelings had developed within me. I wanted to run from the room and never return, to wring Bill's neck for getting me into this predicament. The dumb son-of-a-bitch, I thought, he should have warned me that Pete was black.

Bill stood between us, smiling, all innocence and spirituality,

4

unaware of the fire that was raging within me. I'm certain that Bill wasn't aware of how I felt, for he was the kind of person who only sees the good in others.

Fortunately,, I wasn't completely out of control. In fact, I pretended to be thrilled with sharing the apartment with Pete. Though deciding not to flee was one of the most difficult decisions of my life, it proved to be an opportunity to gain some insight into racism. Of course, I didn't know that at the time. It became apparent during the three months I lived with Pete. I gained valuable insights about myself, my upbringing and how racism infects people, the disease-carriers as well as the victims.

The first week was the most painful. There were moments when the impulse to leave was acute. The reasons that my family and friends put forward as to why I should have remained in New York seemed more and more sensible. Being in Chicago was only causing me grief. And working in a butter factory wasn't my idea of a good job for a university graduate. I was sure I could have done much better back home.

I don't know why I decided to remain in Chicago. There was no rational explanation for it. But I stayed, trying to untangle myself from a web of intense feelings. At first there was a desire to protect myself from Pete. I tried to think of ways to avoid him: perhaps, I thought, by working the night shift while he worked days. But that wasn't easy: as a bus driver Pete was continually changing shifts. Spending weekends at Bill's place wasn't possible because he didn't have the space. I had to face the situation – or depart.

It was a battle I never thought I would have to fight. Not me, the staunch liberal. I stayed, trying to sort out and overcome feelings I had never before consciously had. Although I was frightened, I was also annoyed with myself for being afraid. Rationally, I knew it was wrong to feel the way I did about Pete. But it wasn't Pete *per se* that disturbed me – it was having to live with a Black. Another concern, a deep concern, was the realization that this feeling was a fact, a reality about myself. For as long as I could remember I had committed myself to working for world unity. I wasn't a bigot. I was the guy who always protested my friends' use of racial epithets and their racial jokes. What hurt most was knowing that my feeling about Pete wasn't right and I couldn't do anything about it. It was as if that terrible feeling had been pressed into my being.

The prospect of resolving the inner dichotomy seemed bleak. Seeking advice was out of the question: I was too proud to admit to anyone my true feelings about Blacks.

I guess it was pride – and the hope that somehow I would experience a miraculous change of attitude – that kept me from leaving the apartment. Perhaps being stubborn helped too.

I tried not to think about my predicament, hoping it would resolve itself, but this failed. Pete's new 3 PM to 11 PM shift undermined my scheme of self-deception. During the first week I would go to bed at 10 PM and not fall asleep until he was asleep, sometimes as late as 3 AM. The shortage of sleep took its toll on me physically as well as emotionally. I began dozing off during the day, infuriating my work supervisor. With only 15 dollars left, I couldn't afford to be fired: it cost 40 dollars just for a one-way rail ticket to New York.

I couldn't sleep because I was scared, afraid that Pete might come home drunk or bring home a bunch of drug addicts from the black ghetto where he grew up. When those thoughts seized me, a sense of shame gripped me as well. How could I think such terrible thoughts? I wondered. Yet I did. They sprang from the core of my being. A sense of futility swept over me, for I didn't know what to do to rid myself of those thoughts. They were much stronger than the rational defenses I tried to raise. In the past I had always been able to emerge from a crisis unscathed, but this one was overwhelming me.

During those sleepless nights I groped for answers. While I could distinguish between right and wrong, I was unable to correct what I knew was wrong. A part of me knew that my fears regarding Pete were unfounded, especially since he always came home alone and sober. Nevertheless there was that damned inner voice: 'What about the next time?'

Those long, hot nights produced other revelations. I grew angry at Pete for staying out so late and preventing me from sleeping. What could he be doing at this crazy hour? I wondered. While mentally castigating Pete, I realized that I felt superior to him, more intelligent, more socially aware. It didn't matter that I couldn't prove it, that it wasn't true. I acted as if it were a matter of fact, a natural law, that a Black was inferior to a white. Normally I would not have allowed myself to feel that way. I never would have admitted harboring such a thought. But then again I had never been so close to a Black before.

I really felt I knew what was best for Pete. It didn't matter that he was four years older than I. He could have been 75 and it wouldn't have altered my view. I didn't dare complain about his coming home late, for that would have upset the image I was trying to project. I didn't want him to think that I was like most other whites he knew. I wanted him to feel that I was a liberated person, someone free of prejudice, truly his brother. I wanted him to feel that way about me because I knew that was the right way to be.

But Pete wasn't fooled. I learned that later on. Out of necessity, the persecuted develop a sensitivity of how to cope with subtle and overt hostility, and they recognize sincerity. He never said anything about my true feelings towards him. Through the years he had learned how to make the best of most situations – and there had been worse situations in his life than sharing an apartment with me.

I didn't know then that Pete sensed my fear. I was too preoccupied with trying to face up to what I had learned about myself while giving the impression that everything was fine. That was a torture I hope I never have to endure again. At least a bodily disease can be treated with medicine. But I was wrestling with something invisible. There was no pill to take to dissolve the poison of prejudice in my heart; nor was there a surgical procedure to cut it out of me.

The pressure intensified as I groped for ways to change my situation. Running away, I knew, wouldn't help because you really can't run away from an attitude.

Dealing with racism was one thing, but dealing with the fact that I was so different from what I had thought I was, was just as difficult. I had been so secure and suddenly I found myself confused and gripped by the kind of pain I had never felt before. It wasn't like an ankle sprain or a toothache. Every inch of me ached. Even if I had been able to abandon my body, the pain would have been with me, fueled by a deep sense of shame.

There was a part of me that didn't want to believe what I had discovered. I rejected the principle that recognition of a problem is the first step to its solution. I grew defensive and rationalized that I wasn't ready to endure the pain that was necessary to eradicate my racism. I should be expending my energy on developing my career.

Fortunately, I didn't succumb to that urge. And I have Pete to thank for that. Every time I saw him I was struck by the need to pursue my struggle.

2

IF IT hadn't been for those sleepless nights I probably would have never found what I was looking for. There were so many distractions, so many demands.

While waiting for Pete to come home I could think of nothing but my problem. I needed direction – an idea that would lift me from my fear. Because of my state of mind, I spent most of my time wallowing in self-pity and thinking of how bad I was.

But there was a breakthrough one night. Perhaps, I thought, help will come if I can find out where my racism stems from. That had been baffling me. But where to begin?

I was sure it had nothing to do with heredity. It had to be learned. But not from my parents. They were hard-working, generous people who wouldn't hurt a soul. They never sat me down to explain how bad Blacks were, and I never took a course in school that supported racist theories. Was it my friends? That couldn't be because they knew my position on racism even during elementary school days. I was sure that something must have happened in the past that led to the development of my racism. It couldn't have come about accidentally. Maybe it was something so horrific that in self-defense I erased it from my memory. If that was the case then it wouldn't have been the first time.

I tried hard to recall the crisis situations in my childhood. There were many, but nothing associated with race. Most of them revolved around my father's unemployment during the Great Depression of the 1930s and my parents' gigantic fights.

The persistent probing produced results. But it was nothing I would have consciously suspected. They were seemingly minor incidents in my childhood, minor in the sense that they made no apparent impact on me when they occurred. I must have considered what happened quite natural at the time.

The fact that I had no association with Blacks for the first 14 years of my life created a layer of suspicion within me. I knew they existed because I saw them in Tarzan movies and in the street when we drove through the other side of town. The only Blacks that set foot on our property were the garbage collectors.

When I was about eight or nine some relatives visited us, bearing gifts as usual. At the dinner table, my father, who could do no wrong in my eyes, announced a big money-making scheme that he was seriously considering. 'I am thinking of opening a liquor store in the colored section.'

'Why there?' an uncle asked.

My father smiled and said, 'Because the coloreds love to drink.'

Everyone, including my Aunt Sonia whom I loved deeply, laughed and agreed that my father had a great idea. They shook his hand and toasted his success.

There was another incident that I was able to dig up from my childhood. When a black family expressed interest in buying a house on our block, my parents felt threatened. I remember how our family gathered in the front sun porch, watching the nicely-dressed black couple approach and enter the house across the street. My father spoke openly about his concerns regarding the prospects of Blacks living in the neighborhood. 'It'll become a slum,' he said. 'Our house won't be worth a nickel.'

When my mother challenged him, he grew angry and said, 'You don't understand. I don't have anything against them, but I know what they can do to a neighborhood. The streets won't be safe. There will be drunkenness and drugs.'

My mother was convinced, and we remained in the sun porch

for what seemed a long time, leaving only when the black couple drove away in their shiny new car.

When my father learned a few weeks later that a white couple had bought the house across the street, he took the family to a fancy ice cream parlor where I ordered a double dip chocolate cone.

As I lay in bed staring into the darkness, I tried to understand how those incidents had influenced the shaping of my real attitude towards Blacks. After awhile it became clear how they could have reinforced whatever impression I had already had of Blacks at the time. What amazed me was how seemingly innocent those incidents were; and then I thought of the countless other men and women who had had similar experiences.

I didn't feel resentment towards my father; he wasn't a malicious man. He worked hard to make his family comfortable. Much of what he earned was invested in our house. Not that being protective of one's possessions is an excuse for racist behavior. I simply didn't feel that his ignorance warranted my punishing him. Though my father and I quarreled often, especially during my youth, I always knew that he loved me and had my best interests at heart. I was grateful for the sacrifices my parents made so that I would have every opportunity to succeed. They were good people who often helped others in trouble. I'll never forget the day an old pensioner stopped us on the street to tell me what a kind father I had. My father, who was a plumber, had refused payment for fixing the woman's leaking bathroom pipe.

It was strange, but unearthing some evidence of how I had acquired my real feelings towards Blacks deepened my understanding of what a human being is.

We are so complex, composed of inherited and learned good and bad characteristics that often intertwine and overlap, resulting in mixed behavior. We can be kind one instant and turn mean just as fast. We can love deeply and hate deeply. And we can do things that we resent others doing to us.

11

How, I wondered, could my parents, who had fled Russia because it wasn't safe for Jews, possess the feelings they had towards Blacks? It didn't make sense. You would think that they would have been sympathetic to a people who had suffered for so long. After all, my mother and father had been persecuted, had narrowly escaped being killed by marauding bandits whose idea of a good time was torturing a Jew. And there were the periodic government-inspired pogroms in which Cossacks sacked Jewish homes, whisking away their young women.

The stories of their plight made an everlasting impact on me, undoubtedly awakening my deep concern for the oppressed.

There was always a sense of terror in my father's voice when he would recall the times he and his family huddled in their vegetable cellar, praying that the Cossacks wouldn't find them. How he wished he had been able to prevent the intruders from plundering his house. One thing they never seized was the brass candelabra that his mother used for the Sabbath candle ceremony. It was the only possession she would take into the hiding place.

As a twelve-year-old, my father witnessed – in horror – a band of drunken soldiers arguing over who would be the first to rape his sister. Only the wrath of a Russian Orthodox priest kept them from carrying out their intent.

My father's family – his mother, sister, younger brother and cousin – finally abandoned their small farm. With their meager savings and some basic belongings stuffed into their wagon, they pushed across the Ukraine, heading west for America.

Even after my parents reached the United States, sad news from the 'old world' followed them. In the fall of 1941 my mother's sister and brother-in-law, who had remained in Russia, were burned at the stake by the Nazis after being rounded up with all of the other Jews in town. I remember vividly how my mother reacted to the letter from her nephew that bore the bad news.

Recalling how much my parents endured because of their being Jewish only reinforced my quandary over their attitude towards Blacks. They should have been the first to support the Blacks' appeal for equal status, I thought. Why did my parents allow themselves to be vicitimized by racism? Some insight came during those nights I spent waiting for Pete.

I realized they had had little chance of avoiding the disease. Knowing how hard they had tried to adopt the ways of their new homeland, I understood that they had become aware of its laws and customs, even the unofficial ones like racism. To be a good American, they felt, you had to do what the majority did. Being astute survivors, they sensed quickly what was the right attitude to have and what to do in order to fit in, to be accepted. Though they never talked about it, they demonstrated by their actions that they knew that interacting socially with Blacks was unacceptable if they wished to succeed in the land they believed with all their heart and soul was the most free in the world.

There was another reason, too, for their attitude. It was something they would have never mentioned, not even to their closest friends. They gained satisfaction from knowing that Jews were no longer the most despised in the land, as they had been back in Russia. To them it was a sign of 'getting ahead'.

While I felt confident that I understood how my parents were vicitimized by racism, my problem remained unresolved. Sure, my shame and guilt bothered me, but not as much as the unfairness of my predicament. 'Why should I be infected with racism,' I lamented, 'just because I had no control over my heritage?'

The racist attitude had simply infected me, quietly, without any warning, without my knowing what was happening to me, without my parents – who loved me – knowing that through their actions they had planted within me something so evil.

3

FOR some reason Pete was placed back on the day shift during our second week together. That not only meant that I was going to get more sleep but that we were going to see more of each other.

To economize, we decided to eat at home. Once a week we would draw up a food list and take turns shopping. By the end of the summer, however, we often went to the market together.

Since I wasn't much of a cook – my menu was extremely limited – Pete did most of the cooking, with me serving as his assistant. I loved chopping and slicing things up, even onions.

The guy could have been a chef. He was amazing, especially when it came to making things like gefilte fish and blintzes. Pete had learned to make those Jewish delicacies when he had worked as an assistant cook at a Jewish resort hotel in Wisconsin the summer he graduated from high school. What he made was as good as what my mother used to make. Of course, I never told her that.

Our dinner conversations were pleasant. At first I purposely steered away from anything personal. He respected my privacy too. We often talked about sports. When he learned that I had been recruited by the Brooklyn Dodgers, we drew closer. Though he had lived in Chicago most of his life, he rooted for the Dodgers. Most Blacks did in those days because Jackie Robinson was on that team. In fact, prior to Robinson's entry into major league baseball, Pete didn't have much interest in the sport. He had always been a boxing enthusiast – Joe Louis had been his idol.

Because Pete was black, I assumed he was a fellow liberal, so I felt safe talking politics with him. Pete soon found out that I was an admirer of Adlai Stevenson and that I had campaigned for him on campus during his unsuccessful bid for the presidency in 1952. Though Pete's response was polite, he showed no interest in politics. At the time I didn't ask him why. But later on the reason became apparent: deep down he felt that a Black could never gain political credibility in America. Consequently, he didn't bother with something that had no meaning for him.

At first the only thing we did socially together was attend Bahá'í meetings and have some young Bahá'ís come over for dinner. We looked forward to the meetings, but for different reasons. I was impressed with the racial and ethnic diversity at the gatherings. To me it meant that the Bahá'ís were in sync with their social principles. For once I had found a group that wasn't hypocritical. And it was a religion – something I thought I had shed from my life for good.

I had never been to a place where so many different kinds of people congregated. Not only black and white, Jew and Christian, but rich and poor, Buddhist, Hindu, Marxist, as well as old and young. In a way it was like being where I always dreamed of – my Shangri La. This was especially true at Ellsworth and Ruth Blackwell's meetings. He was black and she was white. Racial intermarriage was rare in 1953, even in the liberal north of the United States. By attending their meetings I grew optimistic about the chances of the human family uniting.

While Pete felt fairly secure at the Blackwell's, it wasn't the racial diversity that drew him back time and again. The fact that that surprised me was more evidence of my racism. I just assumed that all Blacks would crave such a social experience. I wasn't respecting him as an individual, a person with a particular set of characteristics and interests. I was lumping him with every

15

other Black and projecting my feelings onto him. What I thought was good, I felt, he should accept as good too, because as a white man I really knew best.

Pete liked the meetings because he gained spiritual insight there. He was concerned with growing closer to God, whom he loved deeply. It was the Bahá'í teachings on how one attains that kind of growth that attracted him to the religion. Pete, who had need for structure in his life, was impressed with the personal discipline that was required in the Bahá'í spiritual development process. He was searching for a code for living that would strengthen his moral fiber. It was something he apparently didn't find in the black Christian church.

What moved Pete at the meetings was foreign to me. When prayers were recited, not only were his eyes closed, but calm would come over him, as if he were in a different world, one where only love exists. I, on the other hand, couldn't wait until the prayers were finished so we could discuss what had to be done to build a new world order.

Pete and I were different. But our differences, I began to understand, were much deeper than our skin color. He was more deliberate in his speech, more precise in his thinking, and had a greater appreciation for discipline. I was more intuitive, more impulsive and quick to offer an opinion.

After awhile we extended our socializing to the nearby jazz clubs, probably the most racially tolerant places in town. Pete's girlfriend, Cora, worked at one of them as a dancer. At times we would watch her perform with her troupe, and afterwards go to an all-night diner with her closest friend, Ernestine, tagging along as my date. It was fun except for one thing: every time we entered the place, people at the counter and in the booths stared at us. While Pete, Cora and Ernestine didn't seem to mind, I couldn't get used to it. I wanted to tell somebody off or punch someone out. Sensing how I felt, my new friends tried to distract me by cracking jokes or teasing me.

We were all in our early and mid-twenties, wondering and worrying about developing a meaningful career. It was a critical time for us because we were no longer in the stage of life where we could say, 'When I grow up, I want to be . . .'

The women weren't shy about revealing their aspirations. Both were involved in modern dance, hoping that it would springboard them to acting opportunities on Broadway or in Hollywood. In their spare time they took drama and singing lessons at a workshop in the predominantly black South Side.

That I was from New York intrigued them. They wanted to know what Broadway was like and if I had influential friends in the theater world. The fact that I didn't had no bearing on our relationship at all. In fact, they found it amusing that I knew so little about my hometown. I had never been to the Empire State Building, seen a Broadway play or attended a ballet performance. The only thing New Yorkish about me was my accent.

The Korean war was raging at the time, but we never talked about it, even though both Pete and I were eligible for the military draft. Of course, being a university student had kept me out of the army's clutches for awhile. How Pete avoided the draft mystified me. I never asked.

We did a lot of daydreaming aloud during our conversations in the diner, usually talking about our hopes and career goals. Driving a bus wasn't Pete's idea of what he wanted to do for the rest of his life, although his aunt Ophelia had told him, 'You'll never get a better job and the pay is good.' Pete never told us what he really wanted to do. He was private about things like that. One night, however, he surprised us by revealing that he had signed up to take a science course at the Evening Division of DePaul University that fall. Maybe, I thought, Pete's interested in being an engineer. Cora and Ernestine made no attempt to find out what discipline he was pursuing. They just praised him for taking the academic step, urging him not to stop until he received his degree.

Whenever we got together there was laughter. What usually set it off were tales about some of our relatives who had personality quirks, like my Uncle Zonia and Pete's Uncle Josh. Though the two men never met, they had much in common. Both were exceedingly careful about being on time when they had to board a train or bus. In those days only the rich flew.

One story that registered loud and long howls was about my uncle. He had been reported missing for three days. To make sure he didn't miss the Friday night train to Boston, he had left for the station on Wednesday morning, found the seat closest to the boarding gate and didn't sleep a second for fear of missing the train. Not even the police had been able to budge him from the spot. We finally heard from him via a postal card: 'Though the train arrived three and a half minutes late, I am with Hymie in Boston – safe and sound.'

But what received the biggest laugh was Pete's attempt to share an anecdote about his Uncle Josh. Every time he started to speak he would break out in uncontrollable laughter. The only intelligible thing I could discern from his outbursts were the words 'Oh God!' which were really pleas to keep from exploding. Soon we were laughing as hard as he was, even though we didn't know exactly what was setting Pete off. I got so involved that my curiosity about his uncle vanished. And I no longer cared about what the other diner patrons thought about my behavior. At one point I slipped off the chair, fell on my knees, clutching my sides, wishing there were some way I could stop laughing. Seeing Cora and Ernestine out of control as well didn't help matters.

Actually, what Pete finally shared with us wasn't as funny as his initial attempt to tell it. It seems that every time Uncle Josh had to go somewhere, he would tie a string around his thumb with a piece of paper containing all of the travel information he needed to avoid what he called 'unnecessary complications'. His address and phone number were also included – so that in case he was found unconscious, the authorities would know where to ship him.

Cora and Ernestine were astounded that Pete and I lived in such a 'classy' neighborhood. While Blacks worked in the area, none, as far as they knew, had ever lived there. At first they were hesitant to visit us, for fear of being humiliated by some irate white landlord.

Frankly, I was amazed at our living quarters myself. Every time I gave someone my address he would suddenly treat me with greater respect. I guess when I moved in I had been so consumed with the shock of having to live with Pete that I never inquired whose apartment we were sub-leasing. According to my college buddy, the person we were renting from was a Bahá'í friend of his spending the summer in Europe.

After three weeks together, I sensed an easing of tension between us. For example, when Pete had to work a couple of nights to fill in for a driver who was ill, I had no trouble falling asleep. In fact, the first night he was gone, I went to bed unmindful of how I had felt the previous week about his coming home late. It was the following night that I realized I had conquered that fear. But that didn't mean I was no longer infected by racism. That became clear when Pete took me to the neighborhood where he had done much of his growing up.

The first few times I went there I felt ill at ease. Strange for me, because I was a geography buff who enjoyed visiting different places, exploring new sites, learning about other customs and meeting new people. Even though Chicago's South Side was only eight miles from our apartment, it was more distant to me than France or Australia.

I could understand why it had never been featured in the *National Geographic*. Though the magazine published articles about poverty-stricken areas, they were areas that had unusual characteristics like a Mt Everest or a populace that practiced esoteric religious rites. Had it not been for Pete I would have never set foot there. Nothing unusual! I had never visited Harlem either, even though I had lived in Greater New York City most of my life. Oh, I gained a glimpse of its main thoroughfare – 125th Street – when the elevated commuter train sped to my parents' home in the northern suburbs. But I had never had a desire to be down in that street. As far as I was concerned it was a theater set, wallpaper. For me, and the people I associated with, Harlem was off-limits. It was a place I had heard people talk about, and what they had to say was never complimentary. In our neighborhood, if you told someone that you were going to Harlem, they would look at you as if you were crazy, or ask if you had a gun.

The first time I boarded the subway train for the South Side, I actually felt that Pete was my gun. The further south we traveled, the darker the collective color of the passengers grew. By the time we reached our stop, I was the only white in the car. As I stepped onto the station platform I noticed three black men seated on the concrete floor, leaning against a tiled wall, sharing a bottle of red wine. They hadn't shaved for days and seemed too drunk to stand. Above them was a billboard advertising a white wine. A sophisticated blond couple was pictured sipping from the same elegant glass.

Outside the sun scorched the pavement. Thank God for shoes, I thought. But there were children without shoes who were doing what many perspiring adults, including myself, wished they could do. The boys and girls, stripped to the waist, frolicked in the gusher of cool water coming from a city fire hydrant that some desperate child had managed to unlock. Just watching them had a cooling effect. The men and women leaning outside the tenement windows were aware of that. So were those parked on the stoops.

It wasn't only the heat that bothered me. There was an odor that enveloped the neighborhood. The overstuffed garbage cans along the curb, attracting gnats during the day and rats at night, were generating noxious fumes. Evidently the garbage hadn't been collected for days. As far as I knew the Sanitation Department workers weren't on strike. Pete shrugged that problem off as if it were an everyday occurrence. He said he could remember times when he was a child when the garbage hadn't been collected for weeks. The complaints of local residents usually went unheeded by the politicians. To survive, they had learned to live with the stench, which worsened in the summer because of the nearby stockyards and slaughterhouse.

Around the corner, there were shops on both sides of the street. Above them were apartments rented to Blacks by the white men behind the cash registers inside the stores. Ordinarily they were the only whites in the neighborhood, with the exception of the police who carefully patrolled the commercial property day and night.

Pete and I didn't say much as we walked to his aunt's place for dinner. First of all, Pete wasn't the talkative type, and I was absorbed with the sights, sounds and smells of a section of Chicago I had been too scared to visit alone.

His Aunt Ophelia, a tall, slender spinster who wore spectacles, didn't live in a tenement building with ten other families. She lived on the first floor of a two-family beige brick dwelling which she owned, paid for from money she had earned while working two jobs for 22 years. As a child she had learned to be a seamstress on her mother's old Singer sewing machine, which she claimed was the only one of its kind in the rural South Carolina community where she was raised. Besides being a dressmaker, she had worked nights mopping floors at an uptown office building for 14 years. She had left that job during World War Two to work as a temporary letter sorter for the Postal Service, which at the time had had a serious manpower shortage. Though she was never made a regular employee, which would have provided her with hospitalization and insurance benefits, she was never laid off, even when the men returned from the war. She knew that being black prevented her from gaining permanent status. While that bothered her, she didn't allow her anger to consume her. It was channeled into learning more about her African heritage and generating greater pride in her blackness. She had almost every article and book W. E. B. DuBois had ever written and she must have read each one ten times. She was also an admirer of Paul Robeson because, as she said, 'He has guts, guts to stand up for himself and all of the world's downtrodden.'

Despite the heat, Ophelia cooked a three course meal. I had never tasted food like that before. My mother had made chicken often, but nothing like what I ate that day. I could have eaten the whole thing. The crispy, peppery crust made such an impression on my tastebuds that southern fried chicken became a lifelong favorite of mine. So did the thick gravy on the mashed potatoes. Though I normally avoided cooked vegetables, especially green vegetables, I was glad I tried the collard greens because they were a delight, unlike the string beans and spinach I had been brought up on. I don't know what it was about those greens that made them taste so good. What I regretted was not accepting Ophelia's offer of a second helping of her sweet potato pie. I turned it down because I didn't want to make a pig of myself. I had already consumed three large glasses of homemade lemonade.

Food wasn't the only stimulating thing at the dinner table. Ophelia's West Indian boarder, who was a social theorist back home, holding a degree from a British university, fascinated me. The man had a trigger-fast mind and a magnetic way about him, making him a formidable advocate of Marxism. I was so absorbed with what he had to say that I didn't realize the passage of time. We spent three hours talking. Ophelia was as involved as I, for not a plate or utensil was removed. Pete, on the other hand, found Duane hard to take. It was the West Indian's pugnacious manner that irritated him. To avoid a confrontation, Pete excused himself twice. But his control finally caved in and he challenged Duane by charging the Communists with being as vicious as the Klan.

'Both of you advocate the use of force to achieve what you want. To me, how you get something is more important than getting it.'

Duane chuckled sarcastically. 'With thinking like that, man, American coloreds will always be niggers. They're so busy waiting for miracles they not only fail to seize the right opportunities, they can't recognize opportunities when they come their way.'

'What opportunities?' countered Pete.

'There's one right now,' he said, jabbing a finger at Pete. 'And it is so obvious.'

I didn't know what Duane was talking about; neither did Pete. Frankly, I was trying to overcome the shock of hearing one Black referring to other Blacks as niggers. Duane, meanwhile, was deriving pleasure from our perplexity. So was Ophelia, who rarely made eye contact with me. Though polite, she kept her distance, making me feel uncomfortable.

'Duane,' she said, 'tell my nephew about the opportunity.'

Pete looked at me to make sure I wasn't falling apart. I'm sure he would have found an excuse to leave had he suspected my uneasiness.

The smirk on Duane's face vanished when he fixed his eyes on Pete and said, 'All Negro young men like yourself should band together to form a draft resistance front.'

'What?' Pete said, obviously puzzled.

'It is the only just thing to do. Why should any Negro be shipped to a Korean foxhole to sacrifice his life for a country that doesn't give a damn about him, that succeeds in stripping him of his manhood?'

I was impressed with Duane's recommendation and reasoning. Had I been black at that moment I would have dashed into the street to enlist recruits to be a part of the draft resistance front. But Pete reacted differently. 'It is against the law,' he argued.

'Law?' Duane shot back. 'What law? The law that says coloreds must ride in the back of the bus, piss in unequal and separate restrooms? And there are the unofficial laws that keep a man like you from being what he wants to be, from buying a house where he wants to live, and who is viewed as subhuman by whites wherever he goes in this fucking land.'

I didn't know what to think. While I agreed with what Duane told Pete, he was telling me something too, which I found disturbing. But I couldn't respond. I felt trapped, afraid to say something lest I offend someone. I tried to make the best of a bad situation, trying to forget what Duane had just said, but I couldn't. It could be a lot worse, I thought. Duane could have made the same statements to a crowd outside, with me stuck in the middle of it. At least in Ophelia's house I was sure no physical harm would come to me. When I looked at Duane I felt he could see right through me, that he could see the poison inside me. I felt terribly self-conscious and out of place. I got the distinct feeling that I didn't belong there, that my presence was resented. I wanted to be with whites. But I couldn't disappear. Leaving was too dangerous: I wasn't about to walk alone through the South Side at night.

For God's sake, I thought, hide your fear. While I think I did, I couldn't hide it from myself. To avoid being intimidated even more, I finally tuned out of the conversation, trying to gain favor with Ophelia and Duane by agreeing with everything they said.

While riding home on the subway, I didn't have much to say to Pete. My mind was swimming with thoughts concerning what I had experienced in the past six hours. I had been exposed to an anger and bitterness that had been passed on from generation to generation for almost 300 years and which had been rekindled by present day Blacks. Being white and alone with them was scary, and for the first time in my life I began to understand that what I had to endure at Ophelia's is what a Black often feels in the presence of whites.

4

IN TIME I overcame my fear of the South Side. In fact, by mid-July I was traveling down there alone, usually to Ophelia's place.

I'm not sure how Ophelia and I became friends. My guess is that our continual association helped. Perhaps what also helped was my awareness of the need to uproot the racism within me. It became a warning system that kept me from acting superior or condescending towards Blacks. It forced me to be humble. Ophelia and Duane probably sensed that and reached out to me. It wasn't that we didn't notice skin color. It was our humanness that we noticed more. When Ophelia told me that I could visit her any time, I didn't interpret that as some monumental civil rights breakthrough. It meant that she really cared for me. Knowing that made me want to be with her.

Gaining weight that summer, I am sure, was due to my friendship with Ophelia. She knew I couldn't resist her fried chicken, so she would pile my plate with thighs and wings. Her supply seemed endless. I think she derived great pleasure from watching me consume her cooking.

Duane often joined me at the table, devouring as much as me, and at times, even more. He must have had a much faster metabolism than I, because he remained as skinny as the first day I met him. His attitude and manner didn't change either. He was as forthright and bombastic as ever.

I think I was attracted to him because he wasn't afraid to share with others his thoughts and true feelings. He was no backbiter, no back-stabber. I believe he didn't know how to be deceptive. If he didn't like you, he would tell you so.

He was also an internationalist – a dedicated one – something we had in common. It didn't matter to me that he was a Marxist. He obviously had searched for a social system he could align with, and I respected him for it. Being an activist at heart, he became an impatient adherent of his adopted philosophy, trying to recruit the local people into the American Communist Party. He approached his task with missionary zeal because he truly believed that Communism would lead all Blacks to 'the Promised Land'. The fact that he met with so little success infuriated him.

To him the South Side was ripe for mass conversion, for the racism and poverty had – at least in his view – created an atmosphere of despair and hopelessness in the black community. Those conditions were ideal, he believed, for socialism to take root. Though sympathetic to his cause, even Ophelia refused to embrace it. Her reason? 'I can't live without the good feeling I get whenever I go to church.'

When I raised the likelihood of Senator Joseph McCarthy's anti-communist crusade being a deterrent to Duane's proselytizing efforts, he brushed it aside as a 'white man's issue'. 'No,' he said, 'there are two fundamental obstacles.

'Number one – these people actually believe that they will one day share in the American dream. And you can't convince them otherwise.

'They really think they have a chance of getting a TV set, furs and a Cadillac, of one day sitting in a fancy skyscraper office, dictating memos to a voluptuous secretary.

'But the greatest obstacle', he said, shaking his head in disbelief, 'are the churches. There are hundreds of them in the South Side. In fact, there are some being planned as we speak.

'I'm not only talking about the mainstream churches like the Baptists and the A-M-E. I am also speaking of the holy roller churches being held in abandoned stores, in apartment building basements, even behind saloons. And the reason why they exist is because some character thinks that by setting up a new church he will become rich and powerful. They are bloody charlatans, and that includes the ordained ministers. What they give the people is not hope. They drive them further away from reality, making them ill-equipped to cope with many of the problems they must face daily. Looking to heaven for a loaf of bread to drop onto your table is not going to feed your malnourished child.

'Once a week they gather to praise the Lord, singing, screaming, fainting, babbling a bunch of nonsense, with the preacher working himself into a frenzy. And it is in this state of ecstasy that the "offering" plate is passed around, and these poor people dig into their pockets to give their last penny to the church. It is the best con game in the ghetto.'

I was flabbergasted. Being Jewish, I knew very little about Christianity in general, and I knew even less about black Christianity. When I suggested that the churches had some value in providing a forum for catharsis, Duane cut me off.

'I can accept that, but the empty cup must be filled with something meaningful. What happens is the people empty themselves of the anguish, the fear and the anger they have accumulated during the week, and during the next six days the same stuff returns. The smart preacher knows this. He wants to perpetuate this cycle, for without it he would put himself out of business.

'What the churches should be doing is educating the people, helping them set up businesses, strengthening the moral fiber of the people, showing them how to cope with reality. The church should be a force that strengthens the family unit, that provides guidance on how a person can identify his potential and develop it.

'My father, who was a clergyman back home, tried to do that, and the Bishop ordered him to dispense with the social enterprise and return to leading the flock to the Kingdom of God in heaven.

'Being an obedient servant of the church, my father did just that; but two years later he died a broken man, taking to his grave a deep resentment.'

I never doubted Duane's sincerity. Nor his honesty. But one thing bothered me about him. Every time I invited him to a Bahá'í meeting he would promise to meet me there and never show up, not even at the Blackwells'. It must have happened ten times.

My guess is that had the meetings been held in the ghetto, he would have attended them. Suspicious of white people, he rarely ventured out of the South Side. If he did, it was only to go to a university library or for his annual trip to the West Indies to visit his ailing mother and his two married sisters and their families. He was proud of his nine nieces and nephews. Each child's picture was framed and hung in his bedroom, an endearing caption under each.

Duane had nothing to do with his older brother William who came to America penniless in the early forties and in eight years grew wealthy operating an office-cleaning business. Duane considered his brother a bloody capitalist because he hired only Blacks, paying them the minimum hourly rate. When William received a contract to clean several city aldermen's offices Duane suspected his brother of engaging in a kickback scheme.

I was puzzled as to why Pete disliked Duane. Surely, I thought, Pete had to agree with many of Duane's views – they seemed to make so much sense, especially for a Black living in America.

One night while we were doing the dishes together, Pete reluctantly revealed why he was annoyed with Duane. My nagging probably forced him to open up.

'The man is arrogant,' he said, handing me a dry dish to stack.

'But the guy cares for you,' I said. 'He told me so.'

'Maybe it's a personality conflict. But I never could take anyone who had all of the answers.'

'I think with Duane it's a case of having strong convictions. What's wrong with that?'

'Nothing. But I want no part of anyone who demands that I adopt his convictions.'

'I see. You reject his trying to turn you into a Marxist.'

'It's not that so much as his air of superiority. When I'm with him I feel like shit. It's hard enough taking that stuff from my boss at work.'

Pete folded the dishrag, placed it on the rim of the sink and sat down at the table. 'Look, I don't hate the man; I just hate being with him, especially when he bad mouths American Negroes.' Pete swept the salt shaker off the table and into his hand. 'Every time he does that I feel like he's plunging a knife into my heart.'

I hadn't realized that antipathy existed between West Indians and Blacks in the States. But Pete wasn't finished.

'They come from Jamaica and Trinidad, cocky as hell, always critical of us for not taking advantage of the opportunities in America to get ahead.

'It hurts me to see them come here and excel in school and business and seize leadership positions in our community. The trouble is that their attitude towards us fuels the bigots' view of American Negroes. With their fancy accents and English-style education, they can get into places I can't, even though I was born in this country and they're foreigners.

'Duane has no feeling for what our system has done to us. It doesn't matter that he can name every American president, that he has a better understanding of how my government operates. He isn't the product of a society that brainwashes you into believing that you are inferior because of your skin color and where you were born.'

'I don't understand,' I interrupted. 'You mean that you feel Negroes are inferior to whites?'

'Yes – deep down I feel that way. And there doesn't seem to be a damn thing I can do about it.'

'How do you feel inferior?' I asked. 'Because you don't give me the impression of being that way.'

'How?' he said, raising his voice and slamming the salt shaker onto the table. 'When I'm about to enter a train, and I notice the engineer is black, I begin to worry about an accident. I never feel that way when a white man is in the driver's seat.'

That was a revelation to me. Not only because he felt that way,

29

but because he was baring his soul. It was so uncharacteristic of him. By nature he was a reserved person. But then it seemed like he wasn't only thinking of himself as he spoke. It was as if he was speaking for the thousands of other Blacks who felt the same way.

'Ever since I could remember I have had to live with fear. While I tried to drive it from my mind, it was always there, deep inside me, as if it was a natural part of me. There were times when I wondered whether fear and my soul were one and the same.

'Even in safe places like the South Side the fear was still there. There was the fear of not being able to survive, the fear of not being able to find a job, or if I found one, not being able to hold onto it.

'My worst fear was not being able to pursue a desire because of my skin color. That hurt deeply because that, more than anything else, prevented me from fulfilling myself as a human being. I wanted to be a doctor, but I didn't know what to do or who to turn to to realize my dream. Even Ophelia, who I knew loved me, discouraged me by urging me to settle for less.

'I have to believe that she wanted me to do what I really wanted to do; but having more experience of the reality of our country, she wished to protect me from being crushed. I know Ophelia. She wasn't about to shoot craps with my life. She cared for me too much to do that. She knew I didn't have much chance making it as a doctor. Not because I didn't have the brains to make it. She was protecting me from the insults and rejection I would have to endure should I try for it.' Pete paused, then added, 'Now I understand, as Ophelia does, that for us, surviving is more important than attaining.

'In the white world my fear is more intense. It was always like that, even as a child. First my mother, who was a live-in maid and cook for a wealthy white family, warned me about the hostility I'd face in the neighborhood we were living in.

'She was right. Even in kindergarten I learned that I was different. Different not like a violet is from a rose -- more like a flower is to a weed. And I was always the weed.

All my teachers were white. So were my heroes – Superman and the Lone Ranger. The only mention of Negroes was in the fourth grade when some references were made to slavery. I'll never forget the pictures of slaves in my textbook. They were the only colored faces in that book. One picture was of Negroes hunched over, picking cotton with the white master on a horse overseeing them. From my teachers I got the impression that my ancestors were a bunch of savages and cannibals. I think it was in school that I learned how inferior I was to all of the other students.'

Pete grabbed the salt shaker again and squeezed it hard. 'There were nights when I went to bed hoping I would be white when I woke up the next day and that my mother would be white, no longer working as a maid, and that my friends in school would invite me to their houses, and they would come to mine to play. No one ever invited me to his house.

'When my mother died suddenly from a stroke, I ended up at Ophelia's, my mother's oldest sister. That was a traumatic experience. For ten years my mother had been the only Negro in my life. I was thrown into a strange world. I was a Negro but to the kids on the block I didn't act like one. All the kids, even in school, spoke a kind of English I wasn't accustomed to. It took time and a lot of ridicule before I could fit in. But the transformation was made, because it had to be.

'I still feel uneasy among whites. I feel like a stranger no matter how nice they treat me. I feel apart from the scene because somehow some reference is usually made to my blackness. When that happens I feel like a spotlight is on me, with everyone staring at me. Often someone will tell me how great Ralph Bunche is even though I have no interest in politics. When that happens I hear what is really being said: "Man, you'll always be a nigger." No matter what I do, I will always be a nigger, even if I become a doctor.'

5

WHAT Pete dared to reveal had a profound effect on me. Not that some miracle occurred, eliminating the poison in my heart. What it did was reinforce my resolve to get rid of it. It also heightened my sensitivity to what I now appreciate as Americas's 'most vital and challenging issue'. We also grew closer as friends, so close that I was willing to share with Pete how I discovered my racism and what gave rise to it, something I had vowed to keep to myself.

It wasn't easy saying the first few words, but as I got into it, what I wanted to say flowed freely. Pete's attentiveness stimulated the flow. Looking at him, completely absorbed in what I was saying, drinking in information he had never heard before, I was sure he appreciated the fact that racism doesn't only hurt black people. He could sense my pain, as I could his.

I don't think I'll ever forget what Pete shared with me that hot summer night. After all, he didn't know me that well. Yet he obviously trusted me. I doubt whether he had ever opened up like that before, or since, for that matter. Why he exposed to me his truest feelings about something so close to him still mystifies me.

Certainly what Pete revealed opened my eyes to the subtle acts of racism that escape the attention of most whites but which Blacks have to live with every day. For example, whenever we shopped together and I paid the bill, the cashier placed the change in my palm; but when Pete paid and extended his hand for the change, the money was placed on the counter. If we went to a restaurant we were ushered to some out-of-the-way spot, usually near the kitchen door so that we would be out of sight of the incoming patrons.

After awhile I could understand why Duane rarely ventured out of the South Side. He was a proud man. By leaving the ghetto he risked being humiliated by racist acts which would upset him emotionally and which might lead to irrational behavior. With a healthy psyche he could keep focused on his political mission, which he believed would one day truly emancipate America's black people. Pete, on the other hand, as a bus driver, had to negotiate the white world almost every day, and every day he was the target of insults, rejection or – what was worse than anything else – complete non-recognition, as if he were some inanimate object, a machine, a slave-robot designed to do the white man's bidding. While there were no segregation laws in Chicago, Pete learned through advice from older Blacks what he could or couldn't do outside of the South Side. He would never, for example, frequent a barber shop unless he was looking for a shoe shining job. And he would never try on a suit or hat in a clothing store. Hailing a taxi cab was an absolutely futile exercise.

Chicago's unwritten segregation laws finally caught up with us near the end of the summer. Tenants in our apartment building complained to the landlord that we were holding multi-racial orgies, and they demanded that we be ousted from the flat we were sub-leasing. Of course, there was no truth to the charges. We did hold a few parties where Blacks, Indians and whites gathered, but no liquor was served, no one even smoked, and there was no dancing. However there was lots of laughter.

We sensed that some of the tenants were upset with us after a certain incident in early August. Actually, it involved an elderly woman who lived in the apartment below us. What she saw she probably shared with others in the building.

I believe it was on a Saturday around noon when Pete and I invited Cora and Ernestine over for lunch. As we were approaching our place, the downstairs neighbor and her little fox terrier were descending the front stairs. When she spotted us she stopped in her tracks. Though we greeted her warmly, there was no response from her. I guess her feelings were reflected through her dog's snarling and snapping.

The old woman followed us up to the second floor and watched us open the door and enter. A few seconds later we heard her door slam shut. My guess is that she immediately phoned others to tell them what she had just witnessed.

We had 48 hours to leave the premises. Neither my college friend nor his buddy could help us. In those days there were no government agencies to complain to.

Fortunately the day we moved out was mild, with relatively low humidity and without a cloud in the sky. I didn't think of it at the time, but it was a preview of autumn. Our last chat took place on the building's stoop.

It was early morning, before most people headed for work. My suitcase was beside me. Pete's two satchels, which probably contained everything he owned, were at the foot of the stoop. At first we didn't say anything. We just sat there, thinking.

I don't know who started it, but we began to laugh. Obviously it wasn't a funny situation, yet we were laughing. To this day I don't know why we were laughing. The only thing I remember is that it felt good to laugh.

Pete dug into his pocket for his watch.

'What time is it?' I asked.

'About a quarter to eight.'

'When do you have to be at work today?'

'I'll be leaving soon,' Pete said, rewinding his watch.

'Have you found a place to live?' I asked.

'Not yet.'

'Then where will you go after work?'

'The South Side.'

'To Ophelia's?'

'No . . . but I'll find a place,' he said, standing up. 'What about you? Are you heading home?'

'In about four hours.'
'What do you plan to do when you get there?'
'I'm not sure.'
Pete and I shook hands and he headed for the subway station.
I never saw him again.

6

I OFTEN wonder about Pete: whether he ever became a doctor or a Bahá'í. Of course, he could have easily been swallowed up by the ghetto, his dreams dashed by the hopelessness he grew up believing was reality. Whenever I looked for him, I could never find him. He wasn't listed in the phonebook. Even his aunt didn't know where he was. In the early sixties she moved to the Watts section of Los Angeles, a black ghetto with palm trees, possessed of the same despair that plagued Chicago's South Side. As for Duane, Ophelia said he returned to the West Indies when his homeland won its independence from Britain. She said he had never persuaded anyone in her old neighborhood to embrace Communism.

I wish I had tried harder to find Pete. It is something I regret to this day, for he gave me so much. I like to think the little I tried to give him was helpful. Somehow, though, I feel it wasn't enough to make a difference in his life.

I wish I could say that what I learned in Chicago didn't fade when I returned to New York. But it did. Not because I wanted it to. After all, I had never felt more free than when I lived with Pete. For the first time in my life I had taken an honest look at myself. I had begun to do something about correcting what I recognized was wrong with me. I knew I had made progress in overcoming my racism.

But my enthusiasm, my burning desire to rid myself of racism was gone. It didn't disappear as soon as I returned home. It took about a month. Being back in my old neighborhood I was exposed to an environment that spawns racism. It did not undermine everything I learned in Chicago, but it had an effect: the intensity of my personal transformation campaign waned. I think having no interaction with Blacks was a major factor. There were distractions too. I was trying to chart a career, and there was something I hadn't planned on: the courting of a young woman whom I eventually married. Thoughts of my problem were superseded by images of my fiancée and a longing which grew into such proportions that it even impeded my job-seeking efforts. Luckily, a friend's father helped me find an entry-level position with a New York City newspaper. While no Blacks worked there, I ran into some in the field, reviving in me, at least for a while, the zeal to rid myself of racism.

It was my first assignment as a reporter. I was writing captions for a photographer who was covering the 1953 baseball World Series. The Brooklyn Dodgers were pitted against the New York Yankees, a perennial power and a team I had always supported. But during that series I changed my allegiance. The Dodgers not only had Jackie Robinson playing for them but three other Blacks were on the team as well. The Yankees, on the other hand, were an all-white team. I didn't feel like a traitor because I felt that by rooting for the Dodgers I was siding with justice. It also felt good to see the reaction of the Blacks in the stands when the Dodgers won, or when a black player did something outstanding. The black fans' exaltation was really an expression of freedom, a statement signifying their equality with a people who had always dominated them. Without verbalizing it, they were saying to themselves and to the rest of us: 'Look! We are doing what you thought we couldn't do, and at times we can even do it better than you.'

My job with the New York *Journal American* lasted three months, for the army finally caught up with me. It was a precarious time, for the Korean War was still raging. Although news commentators were predicting a truce soon, all I could think about was my involvement in a practice I detested with every fiber of my being. At basic training I was continually reprimanded for my lack of enthusiasm during shooting and bayonet drills.

Though the American armed forces had been desegregated after World War Two, my basic training unit in New Jersey was all white. Hence there was a lack of interracial stimulation to motivate my personal transformation. I needed Blacks around to remind me of my commitment. Without that element, much of my energy was channeled into surviving in an institution I opposed on moral grounds. I didn't yet understand the Bahá'í principle of obedience to the laws of one's government.

I spent considerable time thinking of ways to get out of this military institution I found so objectionable; or if that couldn't be arranged, to avoid being shipped to Korea. My bid to become part of the Special Forces entertainment section, which was an attempt to keep out of the infantry, was rejected. It seems that the officers in charge didn't appreciate my soft shoe routine to the tunes of 'Tea for Two' and 'Once in Love with Amy'.

There was another important matter occupying my mind. It had to do with an unauthorized military project that inadvertently led to my choosing journalism as a career. When I learned that fellow squad member G. David Schine, who had been a close assistant to Senator Joseph McCarthy, was receiving preferential treatment by the Fort Dix commandant, I organized an informational pipeline with the New York *Post*, feeding the newspaper details about Schine's activities. Little did I know at the time that my efforts would contribute to the Senate holding its famous Army–McCarthy hearings, which eventually led to the Wisconsin senator's political demise.

Eventually the commandant learned of my extracurricular activity and I was shipped to Okinawa as an infantry/rifleman. Before I crossed the Pacific there was a four-week stopover at Fort Lewis, Washington, which played a critical role in my personal battle with racism.

Fort Lewis was only about 90 minutes from Seattle, where I spent four weekends with George and Bessie Washington.

How George discovered me still mystifies me. He called the headquarters of my unit. When the orderly told me who was calling, I couldn't take him seriously, for America's first president had been dead for more than 160 years.

But the man I spoke to wasn't joking. The George Washington I grew to love and admire was originally from Georgia. Before becoming a Bahá'í he had been a Baptist preacher and a professor at Morehouse College, an institution that through the years has produced many of the leaders of the American black community.

Though a devoted Bahá'í, this white-haired, chocolate-brown gentleman reverted to his ministerial style of speaking when he talked about his religion. I didn't find it offensive. In fact, he moved me, especially when he talked about Bahá'u'lláh, the Founder of the Bahá'í Faith. It was obvious how much he loved Him. Listening to George, you knew he believed with all his heart and soul that Bahá'u'lláh was the return of the spirit of Christ, that He came to free us of fear and awaken the spirit of love that is within us all.

Because of his faith, George transcended the prevailing sociological classifications. He never said it, but I felt that he never considered himself a black Bahá'í. He was a Bahá'í, a lover of God.

George Washington was truly free, as was Bessie. And their freedom was reflected in their home, a large stone and stucco house that stood high above the street.

The second time I visited the Washingtons I brought along Barry, a white friend who went through basic training with me at Fort Dix. Barry, who had been brought up in a Polish neighborhood in Buffalo, New York, had little experience of Blacks.

That was certainly evident when George greeted us as if we were his sons. I'm sure it didn't help matters that I neglected to tell Barry that we were spending the weekend with Blacks. It never crossed my mind to tell him.

Barry turned chalk white as George led us into the living room.

39

I could empathize with my friend because I had experienced with Pete what he was going through now. I sensed that he was angry with me for not explaining more fully where I was taking him. Granted, it was wrong for me not to forewarn him, and I felt bad about that, but there was nothing I could do. I certainly wasn't going to make up some lame excuse and leave the Washingtons, who had made special plans for us during our weekend stay with them.

At first I thought it was going to be the longest 48 hours of my life. If I knew that Barry was uncomfortable, then the Washingtons also knew. That troubled me. I didn't want to hurt their feelings. I didn't know at the time that they had been conditioned through the years to deal with white folks who felt uneasy among Blacks.

When Barry refused a glass of ice tea – everyone else had some because it was a boiling hot day – I felt embarrassed. I knew Barry wanted something cold to drink because both of us had been complaining about the oppressive weather during our bus ride to Seattle and were looking for something cool and wet to consume.

Mrs Washington left the glass of ice tea on the night table next to Barry's chair. Before sitting down, she told us where the first floor bathroom was, just in case we needed to freshen up. Thank God she did, for I knew that Barry had to go in the worst way – we had been looking for a public toilet after leaving the bus terminal.

Barry remained riveted to his chair. Having been in his position, I knew why he didn't touch the tea or use the toilet: he was afraid of catching some strange disease that he feared was transmitted only by Blacks.

It was a difficult situation. I couldn't direct Barry to go to the bathroom. He was an adult, and I certainly didn't want to embarrass the guy, whom I knew to be a caring, generous person. Everyone at basic training liked him. He had an impeccable character. I doubt if he ever lied in his life.

George engaged us in conversation. He had a way of getting information from people who normally wouldn't disclose much. The way he did it with Barry was by talking to him about his hometown. Coming from a close family, Barry missed his parents and brothers and sisters very much. By talking about them, he forgot his predicament. He opened up, and George listened with deep interest. At one point, George told us that he had a relative who was like Barry's brother Stan – both were ferocious eaters. Both shared a funny story about their kin's unusual eating antics. After a hearty laughing session, Barry excused himself and went to the bathroom.

When he returned, a friend of the Washingtons was seated in the chair next to Barry's. The man was a Bahá'í who had come to join us for supper. Because Barry had been an economics major in college, he was attracted to this economics professor who taught at the University of Washington.

The professor was brilliant, articulate and black. I don't think Barry ever thought a Black could attain such a station in life. We had both been conditioned to feel sorry for 'those terribly deprived people'. Our image of Blacks didn't allow us to accept the possibility of them assuming leadership roles in life. They were to be helped to win freedom, and we, the white liberals, were going to direct their crusade.

Because the conversation was exciting, I can't recall what we had for supper that night. Barry was so involved that whatever fear and suspicion he had when he arrived had vanished. He was completely at home, as was I.

The highlight of the conversation was George's vision and focused enthusiasm. Though in his sixties, he had the vitality of a youth and an optimism that was rooted in firm faith. He shared his and Bessie's plans with us. They wanted to go to Africa, not just to tell people about the Bahá'í Faith, but to contribute something meaningful in a concrete way, to help make the community at large a better place to live. He wanted to set up an agricultural cooperative and Bessie wanted to teach the local people how to can food.

Because of their vision and enthusiasm, I didn't see them as elderly. Normally a man and woman their age look forward to spending their remaining years in a rocking chair reminiscing and watching the days pass.

I can honestly say that getting to know the Washingtons was a major factor in my becoming a Bahá'í. Through them I witnessed how effective someone can be if he truly integrates and puts into practice the teachings of Bahá'u'lláh. Being black in America, and being aware of black history, I'm sure the Washingtons had reason to be bitter and angry. But they were not.

They were new age people. And being in their home was like living in the future that Bahá'u'lláh envisages, free of the fear, greed, despair and envy that plague us today. I know that Barry was affected by the spirit in the Washingtons' home.

George and Bessie went to Liberia a year after I met them and did what they had set out to do. They passed away in Africa, leaving their farm to the Bahá'í Faith.

7

ABOUT two weeks after I arrived in Okinawa I officially became a Bahá'í, signing my registration card one hot July day during a break in a war game maneuver.

Now that I was a Bahá'í I felt I had an obligation to treat everyone as a part of my family. Maybe that's why I found it so easy to get along with the Okinawans and tried so hard to understand their culture.

I visited their villages and made friends among the children as well as the adults. Evidently the elders of the village near our base sensed my sincerity because they invited me to work out with their secret karate society. Its members were the village's unofficial police, coming to the rescue of residents who were being physically abused. Often drunken American soldiers tried to force themselves on local women.

It was my off-duty hours that made my stay in Okinawa worthwhile. I don't think I'll ever forget the school children. The boys loved baseball, practicing and playing games after classes on a field they had hacked out of the bush. The kids were responsible for its maintenance. Considering their lack of tools, they did a good job keeping the field in playable condition.

As a lover of baseball I enjoyed watching the Okinawan boys play because they took the game so seriously. Small in stature, they didn't display much hitting power, but they were quick fielders and the pitchers relied more on control than speed. They were a noisy bunch, cheering their teammates on in Japanese with a sprinkling of American baseball terms like 'home run', 'first base' and 'slide'.

I guess some of those youngsters – grown-ups now, of course – may still remember me, though not because of baseball.

One afternoon I noticed five boys in their black school uniforms taking turns trying to shoot a basketball through a hoop which was about six inches lower than the ten foot regulation height. When they saw me, one of the boys threw me the ball and motioned for me to shoot. I was about 20 feet from the basket – and missed. I made the next shot however. What really impressed them, though, was my dribbling, leaping towards the basket and stuffing the ball through the hoop. All five cheered and urged me to do it again. Every time I did it they cheered, and more people would emerge from the school building, until all of the teachers and students were in the playground watching me do what few Okinawans could do. Being six feet two inches tall helped me perform what must have seemed like a stupendous feat to them.

After I had spent about fifteen minutes stuffing the ball through the basket, a kindly old gentleman approached me, introduced himself as the principal of the school, and invited me to his office for tea. He was familiar with America, he said, because of a five-year stay at the University of California at Berkeley where he studied English literature shortly after World War One.

There were less strenuous encounters with the children. I periodically met with a group of twelve- and thirteen-year-olds in a clearing on a hill overlooking the school. I thought it would be a good opportunity to practice my Japanese but it turned out that they wanted me to help them perfect their English.

They were eager to learn about America, but it puzzled them that a country that was founded as a bulwark of freedom and liberty condoned and defended the institution of slavery for nearly 100 years. It was difficult trying to explain how something like that could happen. It was less awkward answering their questions about Abraham Lincoln, whom they revered. They wanted to know what Lincoln's true motives were for freeing America's slaves and why he seemed so much more compassionate than the presidents who preceded and succeeded him. I had to rely on my sketchy knowledge of American history and on my intuition, because the military library was inadequate. My explanations led to discussions about the existing black–white issue in America. The Okinawans didn't have to go to the United States to perceive the tension between the races. They noticed that the black and white soldiers didn't mix socially, which forced some adjustments to be made in the Okinawan way of life: the local brothels segregated their services the better to accommodate the Americans. And sensing that the whites among their rulers possessed the power, most Okinawan merchants knew which side to favor. So did the peasants.

Incredible, I thought. American racism is taking root in a land thousands of miles from its origin without a conscious effort on the part of the military to spread the social disease. It didn't matter that the US armed forces had been desegregated for about a decade. Evidently there is just so much a law can do to alter a deep-seated feeling like racism.

Personally, what I observed in Okinawa forced me to pay more attention to my struggle with racism, something I had vowed to keep battling until it was conquered. But vows are easily forgotten in the world of the twentieth century. Had it not been for the discussions with the Okinawan youngsters, I would have either forgotten about my commitment or found excuses why I had to attend to other matters instead – practical matters like getting out of the infantry, wondering what kind of work I should pursue after the army, and marriage. For whatever reason, I didn't then appreciate the fact that working at overcoming racism is a practical matter too.

What did astonish me was how all-accepting I was of the Okinawans, an Asiatic people I had never known prior to setting foot on the island. The Okinawans are a short, brown-skinned people. They spoke a strange language, had strange customs, and

45

were suspicious of their conquerors. With the help of the Bahá'í teachings I was able to develop a brotherly relationship with them. We treated each other as equals. We did not need to conceal our true feelings, something I had to do when I was with Blacks – even though they were my fellow countrymen. Being a Bahá'í didn't help much either. My racism didn't disappear when I became a Bahá'í. I was young in the Faith; there was much I didn't know. Being a person who doesn't like to read much was a hindrance, for there are important passages on racism in the Bahá'í writings, which years later I found helpful.

Even when I was with Ophelia and Pete, whom I cared for deeply, I was always conscious of being with Blacks. It was a strain trying to pretend that everything was natural between us. God knows I tried. I was waiting for a sign that told me that the poison I had acquired – unbeknownst to me – was gone. I tried so hard that at times I would force laughter when I didn't really want to laugh, or say something I didn't really mean in order to avoid tension in a situation that seemed volatile.

Interestingly, the only times I didn't feel the need to pretend was at the Washingtons'. It must have been their power of faith that liberated me from my racism during those few days I spent with them. They were living examples of what it means to be fully human.

I wished I had consulted with them about what they did to create an atmosphere where people didn't have to pretend; I wished I could have solicited their opinion as to why I had no trouble with Okinawans while I still felt uneasy with most American Blacks.

In time, after pondering the question, I gained some insight. Perhaps it was best that it happened that way. Having gained it on my own, this thought was easier to internalize. It wasn't a bit of knowledge conveyed by someone else that was filed away in some deep cavern of my brain. This insight moved my heart, which sparked action and reinforced my resolve to continue my battle with racism.

I discovered how difficult it is to undo what has been learned at an early age. How much easier it is to be accepting of a people you never knew before, regardless of what they look like and how they behave, if you are emotionally committed to the principle of the oneness of humankind, particularly one that mandates a complete involvement in living and promoting the principle. When I, as a youngster, was exposed to racist behavior by people I admired and loved, I didn't have such an emotional commitment, which would have shielded me from racism and inspired me with a wholesome vision of what a human being is. Instead, my young heart was penetrated by a virus that grew and hardened over the years, relegating me to a long – perhaps a lifetime – process of chipping away, a process that would require continual prodding. For me that was an important realization. It was unrealistic to expect a spontaneous, total heart-cleansing, though part of me still hoped that something like that would happen. My challenge was to keep my responsibility in spiritual focus. Without it the opportunity to grow spiritually would degenerate into a life sentence of fear and guilt.

8

RETURNING to the United States, I cheered when our troopship approached the Golden Gate bridge. At the time I was more interested in biting into a cheeseburger than discussing the significance of the US Supreme Court's decision to ban racial segregation in schools.

Being back home was great. For the first time, I really appreciated the good things about America, things I had always taken for granted: the beauty of the land, the stores stocked with all kinds of food and the most modern appliances, the variety of newspapers and magazines reflecting a rich diversity of political and philosophical views, the freedom to criticize my government without fear of reprisal, the openness of the people, major league baseball, pancakes and maple syrup, the Statue of Liberty, and the freedom and opportunity my homeland afforded me and my fellow citizens.

Being home and out of uniform was so intoxicating I never thought of the fact that people like Pete and Ophelia, even the Washingtons, didn't share in the freedom and opportunity that I attributed to our country, and that I was benefiting from.

When their ancestors came to America they didn't pass the Statue of Liberty as my parents did in the early 1920s. They were greeted by the boot and whip of their masters who, in large measure, were the founding fathers of the United States of

America. In 1955, even though legally free, Blacks in my country were denied, in practice, the privileges accorded the citizens of our land, as guaranteed in the US Constitution. It was just understood by both Black and white, in both the North and the South, that Blacks had 'their place'. In 1955 only a handful had reached professional status – and the law, medicine and journalism they practiced was confined to black communities. The political, judicial and legislative systems were controlled by whites. There were no black police chiefs or sheriffs. The Blacks had no voice in America's legislatures. Ways had been developed to discourage them from voting. In the South, the poll tax was one way; the Ku Klux Klan's hangman's noose was another. In the North, poor educational opportunities and under-employment and de facto segregation conditions were effective deterrents. The majority of white Americans weren't aware of this inequity; and they weren't aware because they weren't interested in finding out. But even those who were aware merely accepted it as one of those social aberrations that we must learn to accept as a fact of life, and go on with our business.

The absence of collective protest within the national black community didn't mean that Blacks were content with their lot in 1955. Men and women hoped for better times. They dreamed of having what whites had – not only the material things, but more importantly, the opportunity to acquire them. While they deplored their second-class status, and their deep-rooted resentment festered, most Blacks tried to make the best of it. They had no rational alternative. At the time, they lacked the power to break down the invisible barrier the white establishment had constructed, a barrier which separated the races.

On my return from Okinawa, I gave no thought to the barrier. I had no idea that a storm was brewing beneath the apparently tranquil facade of the American black community, no inkling that ten years later the storm would break in the form of race riots which terrorized many of America's major cities.

From my Chicago experience I should have sensed that the storm was coming, realized that the resentment churning within

Pete was a condition that had spread far and wide among American Blacks.

Why wasn't I aware? Maybe because my view was too narrowly focused. I was so inwardly directed, so preoccupied with wondering how I had allowed myself to be affected by racism, so determined to rid myself of the shameful disease, that I lacked the desire to make an effort to grasp the scope of the black–white issue in America. Sure, the celebration of my army discharge and my impending marriage distracted me, but they were minor reasons that made me ignore the black–white problem. My myopic, self-centered view of the issue was the real reason. I had no appreciation of the magnitude of the problem. What I lacked was historical perspective. I was totally ignorant of the black man's struggle in our country from the time he had been forced to come here in chains. Certainly my college American history course was no help.

It wasn't enough for me to learn about Pete's plight, to empathize with him, to learn how I had become infected with racism. Though a meaningful beginning, it wasn't enough.

In June of 1955 I got married. It was a clear, almost perfect day. Flowers were in full bloom at the grounds of the Evergreen Cabin in Teaneck, New Jersey, where the wedding took place. A professional harpist performed. There were about 100 people in attendance, among them a smattering of Blacks, all friends of my wife. The Blacks I knew were in Chicago, and I didn't invite one. Why? I could have said that I was so preoccupied with our wedding plans I simply didn't remember. But the real reason was that I didn't consider my black friends important.

A black woman whom I didn't know very well at the time participated in the ceremony by reading a prayer.

A great Bahá'í teaching opportunity, I thought. This will demonstrate to the guests who aren't Bahá'ís that we believe in the oneness of humankind and the abolition of racial prejudice. I knew that my parents and relatives had never been to a wedding with Blacks in attendance and that it would be a wonderful learning experience for them.

At the time I couldn't appreciate how racist my attitude was. It wasn't a case of harboring malice towards anyone; I actually meant well. My motive was to enhance the image of the Faith. Actually, what I did was to use the black woman as a decoration, a prop to create a favorable appearance. Had I truly respected her as an equal, I wouldn't have done that. To me her only value was her black face. Had someone told me at the time that my attitude was racist I would have said he was crazy.

Fortunately, in this case, the black woman who took part in our wedding ceremony wasn't offended; she was a long-time friend of my wife's family. Had she been the only Black in the Bahá'í community, had she had little social contact with my wife's family, she most likely would have felt used, though probably never complaining to anyone. And if that kind of thing happened to her again and again, she may well have drifted away from the Bahá'ís. No one becomes accustomed to that kind of treatment, no matter how often it happens. There's a limit as to how much humiliation a person can take.

9

AFTER buying a fairly new car, my wife Carol and I felt adventurous. Colorado, with its high mountains, clear lakes and vast stretches of unspoiled land, seemed an appealing place to settle and help teach the Bahá'í Faith.

We set out with enthusiasm but we never reached Colorado. Along the way, one of the Bahá'ís in Tulsa, Oklahoma, persuaded us to stay there to help her struggling community. Not that I had much to offer. I didn't even have a job. For obvious reasons, finding work became my number one priority. When I discovered that there were no openings at the two daily newspapers or the three television news departments in Tulsa, I grew anxious.

In my search I came upon a large marble building with a prominent sign over the entrance, reading 'Oral Roberts'.

It must be a toothpaste company, I thought. A job screwing caps onto tubes would suit me fine. All I was looking for was a source of rent and food money.

When I entered the building, I knew that my initial impression had been wrong. On the lobby walls were large blown up photographs of a man looking heavenwards, his arms stretching to the sky, surrounded by hundreds of admirers. There were also portraits of the same man in an angelic pose.

The personnel officer who greeted me was a woman in her mid-thirties wearing a loose, white, long-sleeved blouse, a long black skirt, and not a hint of facial make-up. After I introduced myself, the woman stepped back and asked with a puzzled look on her face, 'What is your name again?'

'Rutstein,' I said.

'How do you spell it?'

I told her. She then revealed that there were no openings at Oral Roberts.

As I walked to the bank of elevators, someone opened a door and I got a good look at a large room with scores of women behind desks with mounds of mail on them. They were removing checks and cash from envelopes. Prior to calling on his headquarters I had never heard of Oral Roberts, the famous television evangelist.

I think the manager of the small department store that eventually hired me offered me a job because he felt sorry for me. I certainly wasn't qualified to sell socks, ties and men's shirts. But I tried, even though I had a poor sense of fashion.

Keeping the job was imperative: my wife was pregnant. That – and that alone – kept me from following my instinct to quit the job to try to find something that I really wanted to do.

Through dogged persistence, creative opportunities eventually came my way. I was able to sell several feature articles to Tulsa's leading newspaper, I was offered a job as a copywriter with an advertising agency, and I met Thelma Gorham, a Bahá'í and the editor of the black newspaper in Oklahoma City. It was through Thelma that I got to meet Frank and Jim, the editors of the *Oklahoma Eagle*, Tulsa's black weekly newspaper. Maybe it was because Jim was married and had children that he and I never got close. But I think it was more than not having the time to meet: he was naturally suspicious of white people, having never ventured east of Missouri, and living most of his life in Tulsa's black ghetto. Frank, on the other hand, was more urbane, having gone to New York, perhaps the most liberal city in America, to make his mark in the white man's world of journalism. He spent three frustrating years there.

Frank and I became close friends. Through him my wife and I

were able to make some inroads into Tulsa's black community. Having dinner at Frank's parents' home opened the way. No, it wasn't southern fried chicken – much to my regret – but Frank's mother served sweet potato pie, which, surprisingly, was better than Ophelia's.

I wasn't only grateful to Frank for inviting me to be a columnist for his newspaper: Frank's involvement in my life was a reminder of the vow I had made to rid myself of racism. I thought it strange that since making the commitment, whenever I slacked off, something would happen to recharge my interest. At the time I couldn't appreciate where the assistance was coming from. Now I know.

In many ways Frank and I were alike. We were incurable optimists, dreamers who could create exciting ideas and generate in each other an all-consuming enthusiasm for each of them. One idea in particular had great relevance to us: the publishing of a magazine that dealt only with human rights issues. We were convinced that there was nothing like it and that the time was ripe for such a magazine. After work we would get together, usually at the apartment where Carol and I lived. Looking back at those meetings I can now appreciate how therapeutic they were. Both of us wanted to break out of our job situations, to do something more meaningful, more creative, something that would fulfill our innermost yearnings.

I think Frank was more desperate than I, for he would initiate most of our meetings. If we couldn't meet, we would talk on the telephone, usually discussing format and story ideas. We began to make lists of potential stories with a strong human rights content. His list was much longer and detailed than mine.

Our talks were flights into ecstasy: by the time we ended them we were so high that it was difficult to think – or do anything else. We couldn't wait until our next meeting.

For a long time we never raised the issue of how to finance the launching of our magazine. I think we purposely avoided the issue because we didn't want to be drawn away from the fantasy we had created, a fantasy that had become a source of hope for us.

There was, however, a limit to Carol's tolerance. She knew that publishing a magazine required considerable capital and that neither Frank nor I had a chance of getting it. She had hoped that I would spend most of my time pursuing a more practical enterprise – like a good job in my field. Deep down I knew she was right but equally I felt I couldn't give up the magazine. The thought of disappointing Frank troubled me. I didn't want to do that because of a conversation we had had about a month before my first child was born.

Carol had gone to bed early; her ninth month of pregnancy was draining a lot of her energy. Because it was such a pleasant evening, Frank and I decided to talk out on the front porch. We reminisced about New York, sharing some of our more memorable experiences. We laughed when Frank recalled the time he had been stuck in a subway train somewhere between 96th street and 125th street.

It was during his first summer in New York. The train was packed with frazzled commuters and the fans and lights weren't working.

'Being from the open plains of Oklahoma,' Frank said, 'you can imagine how I felt, trapped in the bowels of the earth.'

'How long were you down there?' I asked.

'A long time – maybe two hours.'

'Did it ever happen again?'

'No – because after that I took the bus whenever I could.'

'Buses in New York crawl!'

'That's okay,' he said, laughing. 'At least you know where you're stuck!'

After sharing with each other several unusual experiences we had had in New York, I finally asked Frank why he had left the city. He didn't respond right away. His hesitancy concerned me. Had I violated his privacy? I wanted to take back the question, but doing that would only make the situation even more awkward. As I began silently to berate myself for being insensitive, Frank responded. He stared at his hands, which were pressed against his thighs.

'There was nothing for me there,' he said.

'But it's the news media Mecca of the world!' I insisted.

He looked me straight in the eye and said, 'Then why are you in Tulsa and not there?'

Frank had never snapped at me before. He had always seemed such a happy-go-lucky guy; even his teasing was harmless. I was perplexed and angry. Perplexed, because only two or three days earlier I had explained to him why I was in Oklahoma. But there was a part of me that wanted to strike back – I wanted to tell him off in a manner he had experienced before from bigots. Thankfully, I didn't say what was in my mind during that moment of madness. I guess the part of me that felt bad about my initial response to Frank helped me to regain my composure. When Frank sensed my anger, which I was trying hard to conceal, he changed the subject by mentioning a story idea that he felt was worthy of appearing in the first issue of our magazine. I concurred. The story of how the Indians in the Muskogee area had overcome alcoholism had merit.

'And Muskogee is nearby,' I said, thinking aloud. As I was saying it I was struck with an idea of my own, although I couldn't tell it to Frank.

It was difficult to restrain myself from submitting the Muskogee story to the features editor of the *Tulsa Daily World*. Another good piece by me and I would probably land a permanent job with the newspaper. The editor liked my stuff. While Frank briefed me on the Muskogee story, explaining what angles should be pursued, and how he would tackle them, I was fighting the urge to pirate the idea. The fact that I could entertain doing such a thing disturbed me. After all, Frank trusted me and I somehow felt he looked to me – even though he never said so – to free him from his *Oklahoma Eagle* job, which was for him a professional dead end. It was a responsibility that had been thrust upon me by a set of circumstances I had no control over – and that worried me; for realistically I wasn't in a position to help Frank. Hell, I thought at the time, I am having trouble landing a job with a more respectable journalism outlet myself. On the other hand, I had to try to keep whatever hope he had from dying. The only way I knew how to do that was to continue our talks about our imaginary magazine. Actually, I enjoyed our discussions, not only because they stretched my imagination, but because when we talked about the magazine it all seemed attainable.

When Frank left that night I remained on the porch for awhile, thinking about what had transpired between us in the past few hours. While I had overcome the temptation to run with his story idea, and was satisfied that I would have never resorted to such deceit, I was troubled over my reaction to Frank's sarcastic dig at me. It was the same old demon within me, acting up: racism. I had resented Frank's standing up to me, chin-to-chin. I had reacted like an authoritarian father who had been sassed by his child. But Frank wasn't a child. He was at least three years older than me. That sense of superiority towards Blacks, still deeply entrenched in me, surfaced again. In analyzing my reaction, it dawned on me that though I had never said it, I had, in essence, considered Frank an 'uppity nigger', a term that bigoted whites openly use when confronted by a Black who stands up for his rights. I tried to convince myself that I would never say something like that, that I just wasn't capable of doing it. But then I realized that if I could think it, there was always the possibility I could be provoked to say it. This was hard to accept, especially since I had had a similar reaction with Pete three years earlier. Hadn't I made progress in overcoming my racism? I wondered. It seemed that being a Bahá'í had made no difference. I felt I was in a Dr Jekyll–Mr Hyde situation, for I liked Frank. He had a great sense of humor and we had a lot in common. I always looked forward to talking to him. Even after work, when I was drained, he had a way of revitalizing me. But he wasn't only stimulating company; Frank was my only link with journalism. There was so much to learn from him: he had more experience and a much finer nose for a good news story than I did. My writing improved through his editing of my column.

It was sad to think that Frank was limited in where he could go professionally even with his education and talent. What a waste! I thought. His experience in New York must have been disheartening. As far as I know, there were no black editors or reporters in the established news media in the early 1950s. It didn't matter that there were no segregation laws in New York City and that the United Nations headquarters was located there. The employment pattern of the city's daily white-owned newspapers was such that their publishers could not see the relationship between not having Blacks working in editorial capacities and racism. They believed they were progressive news organs because they ran editorials condemning the KKK's lynching of Blacks and promoted racial integration of schools. While I was at the *Journal American* the only Blacks around were those who swept floors and cleaned toilets. The only way Frank would have been allowed to enter our newsroom during a regular work day was by delivering someone's lunch. Frank's professional destiny was predetermined. No matter how much he would develop as a writer and editor, he would remain locked out of the mainstream newspaper world. Though he didn't want to believe it, I'm sure that deep down he knew that was the case. No wonder he worked so hard to keep our magazine idea alive. I was his wedge that might open the door to professional freedom. It didn't seem to matter to him that I had no connections.

The tragedy is that when I took the job as news director of a local radio station two weeks later, my ability to pursue the development of our magazine began to diminish. I had not had a change of heart, and I still felt the project was worth pursuing, but there was no time. If it had come into being in a flash, or if there had been some guarantee that it would materialize in a month or so, I would have dropped everything else and committed myself to making it succeed. But that didn't happen, and the likelihood of it happening, as far as I was concerned, was nil. I looked upon my new job as an opportunity to gain solid footing in journalism, albeit in radio, a medium in which I had no experience.

The station manager who hired me said he was willing to try me out for 60 days because he thought I had the potential to do a good job. Because I lacked experience, and wanted to live up to the expectations of my new boss, I spent more time in the newsroom than I had to. I was determined not to fail. Consequently I didn't have as much time to talk with Frank as I had had before. I even grew resentful of his calls to the station, seeing them as disruptive. I knew he didn't mean to disturb me, but my insecurity over my new job made me edgy and impatient. Since he probably sensed my annoyance, I tried to make up for it on the weekends; but there were time constraints during that period as well: I needed time to become acquainted with our first baby who had been born only a few days after I had started my new job. I certainly didn't want Frank to think that I wished to end our friendship. In fact I told him during a telephone conversation how much I valued him as a friend, and expressed hope that our friendship would last regardless of what happened to us.

Several days later he came over to interview Carol and me for a feature article he was doing on the Bahá'í Faith for the *Oklahoma Eagle*. He took pictures of us as well. But after the article was published, Frank didn't call as often – maybe because he didn't want to be a pest or maybe because whenever we talked I talked about the Bahá'í Faith and not the magazine. Eventually he didn't show up at the Bahá'í functions he normally attended – informal meetings, picnics and potluck suppers. He wasn't even showing up at the events sponsored by the small group of liberals in Tulsa. He had always been the only Black in attendance.

About a month before we moved to Minnesota, Frank seemed to retreat into the black ghetto. I suspect he finally succumbed to his colleague Jim's belief that no matter what a Black says or does, he will never be accepted as an equal in the white society – all he'll gain from the attempt is pain, disappointment and humiliation. My actions had not done much to alter this point of view.

10

I COULDN'T believe that I had a job as a reporter with WCCO, the leading television station in Minneapolis, a city noted for its sophistication. From my record in journalism, I didn't deserve the job. Furthermore, I knew nothing about television production. But the news director who hired me felt certain that my lack of experience wouldn't prevent me from succeeding as a TV news reporter. It was my social, economic and political views, he said, that attracted him to me. Actually, what attracted him was the Bahá'í Faith, because my views reflected, to a great extent, the teachings of Bahá'u'lláh.

I loved my work. Every day there were new adventures: chasing tornadoes, covering fires and city hall disputes, interviewing famous scientists, artists and government officials from abroad as well as home-grown; and there were the odd assignments like covering a canary-singing contest or reporting the birth of Siamese twins.

I never minded working overtime, even on my days off. It didn't take long before I won the respect of my fellow journalists, including the news director, who called me into his office one day to tell me, 'Nat, I told you you could do it.'

Carol was happy that I had found my professional niche. It strengthened our relationship. A more practical person than I, she felt more secure knowing that I was getting a steady paycheck from a reliable organization each week. That aspect of my job never crossed my mind. I was enjoying myself too much to think about such mundane things. There were times I would come home from work without remembering to pick up my check. That stopped, however, when Carol began to phone our newsroom on Friday afternoons, leaving messages for me to bring home my pay. She was good about reminding me to do important things. Sometimes they were reminders that caused pain, such as, 'Have you written to Frank yet?'

She felt bad that we had left Tulsa without saying goodbye. I had tried several times to contact Frank – twice by phone and once by going to his office – but each time he wasn't around. I left messages for him to call me but he never did. It's possible the receptionist neglected to convey my message, but I doubt it.

I never did write to Frank. Oh, I tried. One night I spent about two hours at the kitchen table, doodling most of the time, trying to think of what to share with him. To write about the weather, the local topography and the beauty of Minneapolis wouldn't ring true, for he knew me as a direct person who had no time for small talk. Actually, I knew what I wanted to write, but I couldn't do it. I couldn't, because to describe my new job to Frank would remind him of his professional imprisonment. The last thing in the world I wanted to do was torture the guy; yet I knew he would be happy to hear about my good fortune. Still, I was sure that my news would force him to compare his situation with mine. I opted not to write. The thought of his being stuck at the *Eagle* angered me. It was so unfair. Here I was, a journalistic novice, working for a prestigious television station which was the winner of numerous news awards, with a staff that was made up, for the most part, of seasoned professionals; while Frank, who was far more talented than I, wouldn't have gotten beyond the station's receptionist if he had tried to apply for a job with the news department. I crumpled up my page of doodlings and threw it into the trash can. Had someone at that moment tried to console me by saying, 'That's reality, Nat, we've got to learn to live with the bad as well as the good in life,' I would have punched the guy in the mouth.

There had to be a change in racial conditions, I knew. But I saw little evidence of that happening, even in the Bahá'í community in the United States. Oh, I had heard about the wonderful human relations work being done in other Bahá'í national communities, where Bahá'ís of all colors consort in unity and harmony. News from Africa was exciting, and from Bolivia. Thousands of men and women were becoming Bahá'ís, shedding ancient prejudices. In India Bahá'ís were breaking down the caste system: Untouchables and Brahmins were serving on the same Bahá'í Assemblies, even marrying each other. Yet in Minneapolis there were only a few Blacks in the Bahá'í community. I felt that was outrageous considering the relatively large black population of the city.

What did the Africans and Indians have that the Americans lacked? I didn't know, but I sure wanted to find out.

At first I thought that perhaps the Africans should come here to teach us. But I knew that wouldn't be a solution, for the American problem between whites and Blacks was a very specific one. All the lecturing in the world – no matter who was lecturing – would not sift the poison of prejudice from our hearts. It was something that all of us had to address head on, honestly searching our souls. And after discovering our prejudice, we would have to commit ourselves to its elimination. A simple formula but not easily executed, as I was finding out.

While I had made the search and commitment, I felt I wasn't making meaningful progress. My treatment of Frank was evidence of that. If I had truly overcome my racism, I wouldn't have allowed myself to be side-tracked by other projects. If I had really cared, I would have made lasting friendships with Blacks. Pete, Ophelia, Duane, Frank, even the Washingtons – they were a part of my past. I hadn't really kept up with any of them. In a way, I had used them to further my objective of ridding myself of racism.

But am I really achieving my objective? I wondered. Have I actually retrogressed in the past two years?

On reflection, I didn't think so. I wasn't doing everything I was supposed to do, but I had taken the first, perhaps the most painful, step: I had discovered my own racism. Further, the fact that I was compelled to evaluate what I was doing in order to keep my commitment was a healthy sign. While that demonstrated to me that I was genuinely concerned, it was no assurance that I had taken any other steps in the right direction. I knew I had a long way to go. I guess my head and heart were not in sync, because I seemed to have no staying power; I was losing patience and even the heart to go on with the struggle. If I could perceive some progress, that would give me the encouragement I needed. But it wasn't forthcoming; at least, I couldn't see it.

What I couldn't appreciate at the time was the fact that the struggle itself is a sign of progress and that the pain it caused was preventing me from realizing it. It was the ploughing up time, an essential phase of the growth process. Without it, seeds don't grow well and the harvest is poor. By burying myself in my work, I had been able to forget my problem.

When we rented a lakeside duplex in Excelsior, we didn't know that the only other Bahá'ís in that town were black. Curt and Millie Ewing had three children: Michelle, who was eight; Geoffrey, who was six; and Tod, who was four. The first time we met I liked them. They were friendly, honest, pure-hearted, hard-working people who took whatever you said at face value. Iowans are generally like that. Curt came from a rural community and Millie was from Des Moines, the capital and the state's largest city. Though they were a few years older than us, we had a lot in common, especially Curt and I. We both liked and had played organized sports. I enjoyed their company because there was nothing pretentious about them. It was so easy to be myself in their presence.

I don't remember the story of how they became Bahá'ís, but I do recall how steadfast they were. That helped me to balance my life. I had become so enamored of my work that I found little time to think about the meaning of being a Bahá'í, let alone be a truly active believer.

I always looked forward to attending the Bahá'í Nineteen Day Feasts, devotional community meetings, at their home. There was nothing ostentatious about their Feasts. Curt was working as a mailman in those days, which just about paid enough to cover the cost of life's necessities. Millie helped out: between household chores she typed labels for a local mail order house. The devotional readings at the Feast were carefully selected, and the refreshments were simple but always plentiful. Geoffrey and Tod loved cookies. As far as I was concerned they could have had as many as they wanted, for they were very well-behaved during the devotions.

I developed a deep affection for the Ewing children, seeing more of Tod and Geoffrey than Michelle who felt she was too old to play our childish games.

I gave the boys nicknames, calling Geoffrey 'Geoffriovonivich' and Tod 'Toderino'. When I first started visiting their home Geoffrey would usually hide, so before doing anything else I had to find him. That didn't take long because he was usually under the dining room table. Everytime I would find him, he would explode into laughter. Tod, on the other hand, would practically leap into my arms when he saw me. So the two of us would end up looking for Geoffriovonivich.

The boys enjoyed playing with our son who was only eight months old at the time. Their 'play' with David was really an attempt to amuse him – funny faces and noises usually worked.

Sometimes our two families would go to Minneapolis together to attend Bahá'í Holy Day celebrations. On the way back – that's if it wasn't too late – we would stop at a restaurant for a soda or an ice cream. It was always fun.

It may seem strange, but I was never conscious of being with Blacks when I was with the Ewings. In fact, we didn't talk very much about America's racial situation. Yet there was something that Curt told me that I would never forget.

Curt was from Boone, where more stock was put on the price of corn and the weather than on global geopolitical intrigues. His was the only black family in town. A good athlete, he was popular at school, and he even dated white women. That troubled his father, who was a devoted husband and parent and considered a responsible citizen by his neighbors. He took Curt aside one day to explain some aspects of his view of the facts of life.

'Black folks and white folks weren't meant to marry,' he warned his son. 'By doing that you violate the law of nature. You don't see a sheep and cow mate ever, do you?'

While Curt respected his father, he couldn't accept his views on racial relations. However, he didn't do much thinking about it until he was inducted into the US Army. In those days the army was segregated, and he found himself attached to a unit made up primarily of black young men from big midwestern city ghettos. It was an immediate culture shock for Curt. He not only found their language, tastes and customs strange, but some he found offensive. It was so bad that he fled the army base without telling anyone – a criminal offense, usually punishable by imprisonment. Curt knew the consequences of running away, but he did it rather than try to live with people who had such similar physical characteristics but who manifested such unfamiliar cultural qualities. He didn't stay away too long however, for he knew that spending time in jail would hurt his chances of advancement in the army; and he saw promotion as the most sensible way of changing his living conditions.

I didn't think of it at the time, but the reason I never felt uneasy around the Ewings was because to me they were simply good, wholesome, midwestern folks. The only thing they had in common with Pete, Ophelia and Frank was the color of their skin. They seemed so secure, as American as apple pie.

On one level, my observation was correct; but deep down, as I learned later, anger was stirring within them, an anger they may not have been conscious of at the time. It surfaced in the turbulent 1960s – the heyday of the civil rights movement. By that time we were living in the East. Though we occasionally exchanged letters and met briefly at Bahá'í conferences, I wasn't aware of the identity crisis they were going through, not until I heard about what had happened to Tod.

For some reason I had always been closer to Tod than to the

other Ewing children. In fact, we named our youngest son after him. When I learned that he had become inactive as a Bahá'í I didn't know what to make of it. He had always been so involved, even as a child.

My initial reaction was to contact him immediately to see what was wrong; perhaps I could help him with whatever was bothering him. But it was a good thing I didn't act impulsively. Tod needed time and space to discover his true personal identity and to become acquainted with his racial heritage. Until his last year in high school he had been on the edge of the black community, a spectator. Having been brought up as a Bahá'í, he believed in the oneness of mankind. For a long time he was under the impression that his classmates felt the same way. But he discovered that wasn't the case; that, in reality, he was living in a racist society. That became apparent when he realized that the only reason he was popular at school was because of his prowess on the athletic field.

At college he was exposed to the black culture. It was an agonizing experience for him. Not only did he learn about the brutalization of American Blacks in both the past and the present, but he had trouble being accepted by other Blacks. This was especially true after he married a white woman. The fact that he and Allison were Bahá'ís who believed in the oneness of mankind was no license of acceptance into the black community on campus. In fact, many Blacks viewed him as a traitor to the race.

His bewilderment as to where he belonged intensified his pain. Life would have been easier had he retreated into the cocoon of the Bahá'í community, where he could have discussed, in relative comfort, the concept of world unity at meetings attended mostly by whites.

Tod rejected that option because he wanted to reach those angry black youth with the message of Bahá'u'lláh. He had to meet them on their own ground.

When he launched his effort, Tod didn't realize how difficult it was going to be to make even a dent in their psychological armor. He quickly learned that he was the biggest obstacle to reaching them; nothing would happen until he could prove to them his legitimacy as a Black. He knew that wasn't going to occur by taking a crash course in being a 'soul brother'.

Tod became a part-time counselor at the black cultural center. His task was to try to help students who had been brought up in the ghetto to feel at ease in the university setting. It was tough for Tod, for he had little experience of such young men and women. It was through these interactions, and other experiences, that he discovered the submerged anger within himself, an anger intensified by witnessing what racism can do to human beings. It wasn't only the bitterness and hopelessness that he was exposed to when talking to the students that made him fighting mad at times; it was their lack of confidence, their lack of self-worth, their hidden belief in their inferiority to whites that was strikingly evident to him once he penetrated the bravado and tough-guy image they tried so hard to project. He was convinced that many of the black students he saw had been emotionally damaged, even brainwashed, by a system that didn't care to take the time to understand their needs, to consider their dreams, to recognize their human potential. And he concluded that such neglect could only stem from a belief that the black man was inherently inferior to the white man and wasn't worth saving.

Tod wanted to shake the gates of the White House. He became an activist. He was appointed director of the cultural center, and this helped him in his crusade to expose the racist practices of the university, and to organize special counseling and learning programs for the minority students who had been neglected by the prevailing educational system.

It was a difficult undertaking because Tod was trying to institute change within a university that felt it didn't have a problem with racism, a university that prided itself in being a liberal institution in one of the most progressive states in the country.

It was obvious to Tod that the university administration didn't appreciate the scope and depth of the problem. They couldn't see with a Black's eyes or feel with a Black's heart. Establishing liberal

67

admissions policies for minority students and giving them financial aid wasn't enough. That, Tod felt, was merely buying peace. Faculty and staff attitudes towards Blacks had to change; black professors and administrators were needed; courses that would acquaint black students with their heritage were also needed.

Tod became a controversial figure on campus. The resistance he met, even from people he respected within the university administration, turned his anger into hostility.

'Why can't they see what is so obvious?' he would lament. The unwillingness of the administrators to see the obvious was what infuriated him most.

To get them to see, Tod applied pressure. Using the news media produced results, especially when he gave them a 24-page document outlining how Blacks were being treated by the university. In time, after considerable negotiation and protest, many of his recommendations were adopted.

But with victory came personal changes. One was Tod's attitude towards whites. He grew to hate them, regardless of who they were. While his hatred was real, it didn't spring from a long-standing aversion. Rather, it stemmed from frustration, from deep disappointment. It was a hatred that could easily be reversed. It was just that he felt that most of his life had been lived as a white man, in ignorance of the black man's history of suffering. And the Blacks were still suffering, still in bondage. Oh, not in chains as in slavery days. It was more that the Blacks Tod knew had allowed themselves to adopt the white man's beliefs, even those demeaning beliefs concerning black people. For Tod, the way Blacks treated each other was evidence of this: the black on black violence, the attitude of the light-skinned Black towards darker-skinned men and women in the ghetto. The more he thought about this condition, the more enraged he became and the more hostile he grew towards whites.

Tod's marriage suffered from his struggle to discover who he really was. He and his wife separated. His agony was compounded when he could not see his two young daughters every day.

It seems the angrier Tod and other Blacks on campus became, the more respect Blacks gained there. But Tod knew that it wasn't a respect based on equality. It was based on fear, fear of rioting and what a riot could do to an order white people found comfortable and wanted to preserve at all cost.

For about two years Tod was single-minded in his determination to generate greater self-respect and confidence among minority students, to try to uncover and eradicate every trace of racism on campus. It was an impossible task for one man and Tod knew it. But he had to do something to change the way Blacks were being treated in his little part of the planet.

With most of his energy channeled into his mission, Tod gradually became inactive as a Bahá'í. For two years he didn't attend meetings and he avoided white Bahá'ís, even some of his close friends. Yet with all of his pushing, his maneuvering and clawing, he never lost his love for Bahá'u'lláh. Despite his newly-acquired antipathy towards whites, deep down he believed in the oneness of humankind, the most important social principle of his Faith. As a child and youth he had witnessed men and women earnestly trying to practice that principle at Bahá'í gatherings. How could he ever forget those meetings and what he had learned in the children's classes? Through them he had developed a vision of what humanity was destined to be like: men and women, black, white, yellow and brown living and working together, knowing that they belonged to the same family, the family of man. That vision had been pressed into his consciousness. The fact that it wasn't yet a reality disturbed him. He wanted it to be realized immediately so that he would no longer have to push, maneuver and claw to get his programs approved. He didn't like the aggressive stance he had to take but no one else was willing to fight with the intensity that was necessary to achieve what had to be done.

Talking about his vision with either Blacks or whites was a wasted effort. They hadn't experienced what he had as a child and they couldn't appreciate what he saw and felt. They brushed it aside as 'wishful thinking'. While there were times when he turned his back on the vision, it never vanished. That turned out to be a blessing, because whenever things weren't going well at the cultural center he would resort to prayer and his vision of a united world would come to mind.

It was a good thing for Tod that he didn't reject his Faith and its reliance on prayer, because even though Blacks on campus were receiving better treatment and were gaining greater confidence – which was helping them earn higher grades – they were growing more hostile towards whites. And the whites, in turn, were becoming annoyed with the sudden assertiveness and aloofness of the Blacks. Consequently, whites avoided Blacks wherever they congregated, including the cultural center.

The polarization along racial lines disturbed Tod. He hadn't planned on that happening. The black–white chasm on campus had widened, and there was nothing the university or the local and state governments could do to bridge the social gap.

Though the unexpected turn of events was unsettling, Tod knew that social progress doesn't come easily. But he also knew that there was always the possibility of things getting out of hand, that there could even be violence. That realization forced Tod to draw on the spiritual resources he had developed as a child and youth. It was that action that drove him to readjust his thinking about white people. He began to work for unity, not only between Blacks and whites, but of all people. Tod began reading Bahá'í books again and seeking out those individual Bahá'ís he had snubbed. He sensed that he was becoming spiritually rekindled – and that felt good. His mood began to lighten and he was able to become more detached from his work. Tod returned to his wife and daughters a stronger person and with a more honest sense of himself.

He had no misgivings about what he had done, for it had been long overdue. For the first time Blacks and other minority students were feeling good about themselves; they could learn about their heritage and attend classes taught by non-whites. But Tod realized that this was only the first step in the right direction, that eventually the minority students would have to travel the course that leads to the unification of mankind. And be believed that that would happen one day.

His involvement with the cultural center was personally rewarding. While working there he discovered his blackness and thereby found out something about himself that he had never known before.

Shortly after announcing his resignation from the center, Tod received a pleasant surprise – a call from the university president, who had also grown wiser during the five-year struggle. He offered to write Tod a letter of recommendation. For Tod that was a positive sign. It convinced him that the administration had finally recognized that his effort to apprise them of the racial problem on campus had had merit after all.

11

AFTER 14 months at WCCO, I decided I was ready for the big time –
one of the three news networks based in New York City.

The drive back East was horrendous. All of our possessions
were piled into the back of our 1955 Nash-Rambler stationwagon,
with our 20-month-old son strapped into his 'potty' chair on top
of the pile.

As we drove through Wisconsin, I tried to reassure Carol that
we were making the right move, that I was sure of landing a job in
New York. Before leaving she had reservations about moving
across the country, for we had established some security in Minnesota and had made some strong friendships there, especially with
the Ewings. Also, moving while in her fourth month of pregnancy was an added hardship. But she was game. Knowing that
we would soon be with our families and old friends lessened
some of the anxiety.

When we reached Indiana, we were greeted by a blizzard that
stayed with us for nearly 200 miles. Compounding our visibility
problem was the loss of our automobile lights at night somewhere
in central Ohio. The only way we could make it to the next
turnpike exit, which was 15 miles ahead, was to follow the tail
lights of the huge truck in front of us. Fortunately, there was a
motel about 300 feet from the exit ramp.

The first week home was one grand reunion. The next week,

however, a telephone follow-up to my earlier postal inquiries to the network news departments about possible jobs produced negative results. I began to scramble, looking for a job anywhere, for I had a family to feed and a house to keep; and in five months we would have another child.

It wasn't long before I got a reporter's job with a new newspaper in Port Chester, New York. It was about 20 miles north of my parents' place where we were staying until I could find a job that would pay enough for us to establish a home of our own. The job only paid $100 a week.

Carol said she would go to work to help out; but she couldn't do it right away because she miscarried just before reaching her fifth month of pregnancy. The whole episode shattered me. I blamed myself, for had we remained in Minnesota the tragedy could have been avoided. On the day of Carol's miscarriage I flirted with the idea of calling WCCO to see if I could get my old job back; and I must have made 30 phone calls to radio stations and newspapers in a 50-mile radius of New York City to try to get a better job. There was not one positive response. It was then that I discovered the power of prayer, an aid I would later rely on in battling my racism.

About a week later we received a call from my in-laws asking if Carol and I would spend the weekend with them; they wanted me to meet their friend and guest William Sears, who had been a famous American TV personality prior to moving to Africa to help further the Bahá'í cause there.

It was during a breakfast conversation that Mr Sears offered to contact his TV news director friend in Philadelphia on my behalf.

About three weeks later I was producing the '11th Hour News' at an NBC-owned and operated station in Philadelphia. It was here that over the next three-and-a-half years I would gain deeper insights into America's black–white issue.

We moved into the Germantown section of the city because a friend offered us an apartment in one of his buildings at a reasonable rate. Before we moved there we didn't know that the neighborhood was predominantly black. We would not have avoided the place had we known – it was just that neither of us had ever lived in such an area before.

The apartment was much nicer than anything we had lived in in Tulsa or Minnesota. The rooms we occupied had at one time been a section of an elegant mansion that in recent years had been converted into a four-apartment dwelling. I had never lived in a place with such high ceilings. They were at least 12 feet high. Through the parlor's French doors was a balcony facing the street.

Since I had a regular work schedule, I decided it was possible to use public transportation to get to and from work. To reach the TV studio, I had to take a bus to a subway station, where a train would transport me to about three blocks from where I worked. The entire route was thickly populated by Blacks with the exception of the ritzy Rittenhouse Square section in the center of the city, not far from the television station. At the time I never worried about the commute, even though I was traveling home around midnight. I can't provide a rational explanation for my lack of fear, other than that my experience in Chicago's South Side had familiarized me with life in the ghetto. I already knew that the majority of people living there were hard-working men and women who were trying to improve their lot, many of them hoping one day to own their own home in the suburbs.

There were a number of Blacks in the Philadelphia Bahá'í community, two of whom served on its elected nine-member governing body, the Local Spiritual Assembly. While Helen Underhill and I became friends, I was much closer to David Penn. Whenever I think of him I'm reminded of how beautiful a human being can become. Though he didn't earn much money as a post office worker, David managed to support several Bahá'ís who were serving the Faith abroad. He never knew that I was aware of his quiet generosity. I don't think I ever heard David say an unkind word to anyone, or about anyone. When in his presence I felt completely at ease; I felt spiritually embraced by him.

I can understand why my eldest son, who was four at the time, was attracted to David. One day while outside he took hold of

David's hand and studied it, then stroked his face and finally asked, 'Why are you brown all over?'

David put his arm around my son and pointed to the patch of flowers growing alongside the foundation of the building where we were living. He said, 'See, flowers are like human beings – they come in different colors. God made it that way so that life would be more beautiful. How dull it would be if everyone looked and acted alike.'

The boy took David's hand and led him inside our apartment to his room where he showed off his latest toy – a big brown teddy bear. Then he collected his black and his white teddy bears and placed all three on David's lap. The child stepped back to survey what he had done and grinned.

For awhile I thought I had overcome my racism. The black–white relations in the Philadelphia Bahá'í community seemed so smooth, so free of tension, and I felt perfectly comfortable in it. In fact, I felt proud of its racial make-up and of how well everyone got along together. As far as I was concerned there wasn't another group in the city that was as thoroughly integrated as the Bahá'ís. I felt confident that my observation was accurate because as a journalist I had a fairly good idea of the city's social composition.

But my triumphal feeling soon vanished because of an incident that took place between our landlord's son and mine. I soon realized that to me the incident was more than a typical kid's scuffle, one that sets off hurt feelings one day and is forgotten the next.

Stevie, who teased and struck our son, was black even though his father, Cliff, couldn't admit it at the time. Cliff was a member of the Bahá'í community and I remember when he first introduced Stevie to us, he said then, in all seriousness, that his wife's parents were from southern Italy and that the Moorish influence there must have rubbed off on his son.

I didn't believe Cliff's explanation but neither did I dwell on the fact that Stevie was black. It didn't seem to make any difference to me, that is, not until Carol told me what Stevie had done to our son. My dormant racism erupted. The little black bastard, I thought. I wanted to strike Stevie; and it wasn't only because I wanted to protect my child. The impulse sprang from that monstrous thing that had me in an unbreakable stranglehold. I was at a loss. 'How could that sick thought come to mind after what I experienced in Chicago and Tulsa?' I wanted to cry out.

As I grew more remorseful I sensed that I was heading into another episode of emotional self-flagellation. But thank God that was avoided when a thought struck me: 'Use your Faith!'

I prayed. I prayed with such openness and honesty that I did something I had never done before – in fact, in my college days I had mocked people who did it. I fell to my knees, beseeching God for help. Space and time were no longer factors. I knelt in silence, devoid of self, of any personal thought. It was as if someone had lit a candle in the darkness: I saw a solution to the Stevie issue. The next day I called on his mother and calmly discussed what went on between our sons. On that same day the boys were playing together again. Of course, in time they had other arguments and scraps, but they always managed to sort them out and remain friends.

I grew to love Stevie and his father because of the courage they demonstrated in their struggle with the pressures of racism. Like many people, they suddenly awakened to the fact that they had been direct victims of the disease for a long time. How they dealt with racism has been the source of inspiration to me over the years. Through their tests and trials I gained more insight into how racism wreaks havoc with the human spirit and warps community development.

Cliff's college-educated uncle usually asked his parents whenever they met, 'Does Cliff still have that nigger kid?' Cliff knew his family's attitude and it bothered him some, but it never lessened his love for his youngest son. Even when Cliff discovered that he hadn't fathered Stevie, which he found out when the boy was four, he never wavered in his role as father to the youngster. Their relationship grew stronger despite the agony they had to endure in order to preserve their father–son connection in a society that, for the most part, finds racial mixing repugnant.

When Cliff and his wife divorced Stevie stayed with Cliff. In many ways, Cliff functioned as the child's mother and father, making meals, cleaning house and washing clothes. Of course, Cliff's older son and daughter helped out with household chores, too.

Cliff didn't enjoy the domestic responsibilities, but they had to be done. He was determined to maintain a harmonious home for his children, even though there was no mother around. That was difficult to do, especially when he had to earn a living and wanted to continue his writing, something that he had to keep up in order to satisfy his insatiable need for creative expression. He had published a number of articles and short stories and was working on a novel. People whose literary judgment he valued considered Cliff extremely talented. Most of his writing was done when the kids were asleep or off playing with friends.

While Cliff enjoyed writing because it satisfied a deep creative urge, I think he was also drawn to his pen because it was a way to escape. One of his greatest worries was what was going to happen to Stevie. There were many nights when Cliff stayed awake trying to think of possible solutions to that problem. Stevie, he thought, would one day want to meet his biological father. And he would undoubtedly find it difficult to determine where he belonged. Would it be in the black or white community? Or would he be accepted by both, or rejected by both?

At four, the child began to ask questions. One day while leaving a movie theater, Stevie pointed to his arm and asked Cliff, 'Why am I this color and you're not?'

While Cliff tried to answer the question, he doubted whether Stevie understood what he was trying to say to him. The youngster wanted to be exactly like the man he loved most in the world, but in this one way he couldn't. That was an emotional hurdle Stevie would probably have trouble clearing for the rest of his life.

The pain from the wounds inflicted upon Stevie were felt by Cliff as well. That came early in the child's life. As soon as he made friends in the neighborhood, he started running home, crying, 'They keep calling me "black boy" and I'm not.'

Then there was ridicule in school, especially from black children who viewed Stevie as an oddity because he looked black but acted white. Cliff was desperately trying to find ways to solve his son's identity crisis. It was playing havoc with the child's formal education. Stevie was expelled from an excellent private school because his teachers felt he had serious emotional problems. Sending him back to the public school, Cliff felt, was like casting a capon into a den of hungry wolves.

Cliff wanted to run away with Stevie and his two other children and live somewhere in the mountains, where he could educate his youngest son himself. Society seemed so cruel and uncaring. It was destroying Stevie. The only place where the boy felt at ease outside of his home was in the Bahá'í community. Because of that, Cliff tried to take the youngster to as many meetings as possible. Spending a week at Green Acre Bahá'í school in Maine in the summer thrilled Stevie, for he felt free there. He wasn't stared at, wasn't judged. This reinforced Cliff's faith; it also reconfirmed his belief that Stevie wasn't a misfit, as some school psychologists claimed. Given the right environment, Cliff knew the child would blossom. The only time when Stevie would display displeasure at a Bahá'í meeting was when people assumed he was David Penn's son. Stevie, Cliff and David would often go to Bahá'í meetings together.

How to help Stevie was a question that continued to plague Cliff. Spending an hour or two with the local Bahá'ís or a week at Green Acre once a year wasn't enough to protect his son from the daily behavior of black and white people who have a warped understanding of race. Isolating him wasn't the answer; but allowing him to be chewed up psychologically by an insensitive system wasn't right either.

After school hours Cliff, his son John and daughter Louise tried to help Stevie with his homework, especially his mathematics lessons. While he had difficulty grasping that subject, Stevie would continually tell his father and brother and sister, 'I know

I'm not dumb.' Cliff soon realized that he and his older children didn't have the skills to undo the damage that Stevie's teachers and fellow students had inflicted on him. The fact that the youngster believed that he wasn't stupid, and that his father and brother and sister reinforced that belief, kept him from being devoured by a life-long feeling of inferiority. Some professional counseling helped also. But what helped most was Cliff's continuous showering of love upon the child. Of course Stevie reciprocated, which caused an indissoluble bond between the two, a bond that never broke, even during Stevie's traumatic adolescence when he was drawn to marijuana for awhile, and dropped out of high school. The more trouble Stevie got into, the closer Cliff was drawn to him. He taught him his trade – piano tuning – and encouraged him to master the guitar. In time, Stevie went to night school to finish high school and then went on to college to become an occupational therapist for the emotionally disturbed. And he became a devoted Bahá'í.

The relationship that Cliff and Stevie forged helped others. One day John, who had become a doctor, approached his father and said, 'Dad, you'll never know what it means to me to have a black man as my brother.'

Years later, Cliff's ex-wife met him at a social function and told him, 'I'm extremely grateful for what you did for Stevie, and I'm happy that he's a Bahá'í.' But what touched Cliff the most was when Stevie – a grown man at the time – approached him one day and said, 'You were the only father I ever knew, and you were always there when I needed you.'

Cliff admits today that he remains emotionally closer to Stevie than to his other children. And now that the long trail of tears and pain that resulted from the struggle is gone, he can better assess how he benefited from the 25-year struggle. By being close to Stevie, he gained a deep appreciation of what black people must endure to survive in a society that is fundamentally racist. By being with Stevie all those years, Cliff eventually realized that the black man's cry for equality is really a cry to be recognized as a human being.

12

BY THE early 1960s I had a lot to be grateful for: I was working for a leading national network news department based in New York City, we had purchased our first home in suburban New Jersey, and we had four healthy children.

But one thing hadn't changed: I was unable to discern any change in that thing that was haunting me – my racism. Moving from place to place didn't seem to have any effect on it. If I had made any progress I was incapable of perceiving it. On the other hand, if being more knowledgeable about the black–white issue, more sensitive to its impact on people counted, then perhaps I had made some progress. But deep down I knew this kind of advancement was superficial at best. That uneasy feeling towards Blacks remained intact. During private moments, when all alone with my thoughts, I would wonder whether what had been pressed into my heart could ever be removed. Such thoughts depressed me; they had a paralyzing effect. I couldn't generate the will to become involved in social action efforts that promoted community racial harmony. Yet as a Bahá'í I knew I had a responsibility to overcome whatever prejudices I had and to work for greater unity wherever I lived and worked. Reminding myself of that would usually lift me out of the doldrums; but it wasn't as simple as pressing some spiritual button that's guaranteed to alter one's attitude immediately. Through the years I had learned that acceptance of a principle is no guarantee that you will act on it. Help is usually required. In my case that was forthcoming. At first, I never questioned how the help materialized; that would become clear years later. In the meantime, when the social action opportunities came my way I tried to take advantage of most of them, though not all proved fruitful.

When my sister informed me of a special committee being formed in town to help Blacks move into white residential sections, I attended the group's first meeting. I was aware of the local real estate establishment's policy of not selling property to Blacks in white neighborhoods, rich or poor. All the Blacks – about ten families – lived in a small area bordering on the railroad tracks and a box factory.

About 30 men and women showed up at the meeting. I was particularly impressed with a young rabbi who spoke eloquently about the need to break down all racial barriers in town. He was also a doer. The rabbi had contacted a nearby chapter of the National Association for the Advancement of Colored People to organize a test case in town. A black couple who wanted to purchase a house in a white neighborhood had been chosen and were at the meeting. The rabbi had brought them there.

A week later, at an organizational meeting, I was asked to be the committee's Executive Director. Frankly, I was surprised that I had been chosen, because I was a newcomer. The rabbi, I felt, should have been appointed to the position. The fact that he wasn't bothered me. I knew it had nothing to do with anti-Semitism, because about half of the committee members were Jewish and part of his congregation.

Needless to say, I was enthusiastic about the prospects of the committee overcoming a long-established evil in town. All sorts of sub-committees were set up: publicity, real estate relations, education, funding, membership and social. On paper the committee seemed equipped to achieve all its goals. Several lawyers, teachers, psychologists and a doctor belonged to the group – and they all seemed committed.

Unfortunately, we didn't accomplish much. In fact, the test

case was never tested. Not that the black couple backed out – our committee's enthusiasm petered out. The sub-committee on real estate relations never met with the town's real estate firms. The sub-committee tried once, and when it failed to arrange a meeting, the members seemed to lose interest. Only the social sub-committee met regularly. Its end-of-the-year party was hailed as a smashing success. While not one black person attended the affair, almost every committee member showed up, dancing and drinking till past midnight.

At several meetings I appealed to the members to become more involved in their sub-committee work. I thought I had reached them because after my pep talks some would make it a point to tell me how I had inspired them. But the next day they acted as if they hadn't attended the meeting and between meetings they did little or no committee work. I was becoming disheartened, and the rabbi sensed it.

One evening after presiding over another frustrating meeting, the rabbi approached me and whispered, 'They aren't committed. They really don't want to achieve the goals of the committee. They belong because they think it's fashionable to belong. These days lots of people who consider themselves liberals think it is fashionable to be involved in the civil rights movement, especially as it gets lots of exposure on TV.'

Several months later we moved away, finding a place that was closer to New York and more racially balanced. The latter was especially important to us because we wanted our children to live among people of color.

While nothing meaningful resulted from my Fair Housing Committee experience, an opportunity to do something constructive for the civil rights cause surfaced at work. NBC hired a black man who had been a reporter with the *New York Times* and two young black men as news researchers. I'm not sure what motivated the network to do it. My guess is that they wanted to be in sync with the spirit generated by the passage of the historic civil rights legislation.

I felt I should try to make the Blacks as comfortable as possible, because they would be working in a place where Blacks had never worked before. No matter how well-meaning the entrenched work force might be, they could unwittingly hurt the new journalists during the course of the day. After all, very few of us had experience interacting as equals with Blacks on a daily basis.

Mistakes were made. The ones that stand out most in my mind were the ones I made. I was too eager to help, acting as if I had been chosen to carry on a special human rights mission.

The new staff members appreciated my introduction of them to the news department but my offer to advise them on how to handle the journalistic demands that are peculiar to television was rejected. The reporter wasn't as polite as the researchers in their rejection. He actually bristled. I didn't realize at the time that I had been patronizing. I had assumed that he was ignorant of how to write filmscript, and without asking whether he wanted my advice, I gave it in a fatherly fashion.

When he rejected my offer, I bristled in turn. Why does he have such a chip on his shoulder? I fumed. I was only trying to help him – how ungrateful!

I avoided the reporter for a week, for I had never been slighted like that by a black person before. The guy had verbally slapped me down. It wasn't so much what he said that bothered me. After all, the wording wasn't offensive in any way: 'No thanks!' he had said. 'I can handle it.' But the narrowing of his eyes and the gritting of his teeth after uttering those words conveyed a different message. What he really meant was, 'You can take your offer and shove it.' I was sure that's what he really said to me. And every time I thought about it the blood within me boiled.

Puzzled, I consulted with Carol about the incident. To her it was no great mystery as to what happened.

'Honey,' she said, 'he rejected your offer because he felt that you were condescending.'

'How?' I asked. 'I was only trying to help the guy.'

'I know, but I think you were assuming that he was ignorant of something that you had no proof he was ignorant of. You took the position of the learned one, making him feel like the unlearned one.'

'I was acting like the benevolent master, wasn't I?'

'Honey, I suspect that's what he felt – and he recoiled.'

Carol's interpretation made sense. The next day I sought the reporter out and apologized. He appreciated that, and we became friends. After getting to know him better, I cringed every time I reminded myself of what I had done. For the guy was not only a solid journalist, but he was a skillful filmscript writer. It was something he had mastered while working at a TV station in Wisconsin.

It was during my stay at NBC News that Americans of African ancestry began to describe themselves as Blacks. The terms Negro and colored were scrapped.

The 1960s was a tumultuous time. The Blacks' restrained call for freedom burst into a cry heard nationwide, a cry punctuated by hurled molotov cocktails exploding in streets, by the burning of whole city blocks, and by the looting of white-owned property. 'Black is beautiful' became the rallying cry of young black men and women across the land.

Whites, from politicians to factory workers, felt threatened. Their fears weren't imaginary because they either experienced, or saw on television, cities burning, even sections of Washington DC. Millions watched on TV as police dogs attacked little black children on their way to church, the corpses of black and white civil rights workers being pulled out of a Mississippi ditch where they had been dumped by the Ku Klux Klan.

We saw black college students being beaten over the head because they tried to integrate a diner. We saw governors trying in vain to block black students from entering state universities; armed US troops had to pave the way. We saw state troopers, mounted on horses, wielding clubs and cattle prods, charging into freedom marchers led by Dr Martin Luther King in Selma, Alabama. We saw Dr King's march on Washington DC, where he shared his most precious dream with a nation reeling from a social convulsion that many felt was long overdue. His dream was a dream that others in the past possessed but didn't dare express. It was a dream that didn't die when a bullet tore through him. There were too many people – black and white – who had personally embraced his dream as a message of hope to let it die. They couldn't imagine it remaining unfulfilled because they wanted to believe that it was an accurate reflection of America's destiny.

As a journalist covering the civil rights struggle during the 1960s, I saw things that many laymen didn't. There were incidents that the TV cameras didn't record, incidents that made me doubt whether racism was being tackled, never mind eradicated, in America, despite the sacrifices and heroic efforts made by some. God knows, I didn't want to accept what I felt. Yet my doubts persisted, for the evidence was clear. Little things happened that caught my attention. Whether other journalists noticed what was happening I don't know. What I do know is that I'll never forget what I saw.

Idealistic, well-meaning white men and women went south to help organize black voter registration campaigns. In their desire to further the cause, some volunteers revealed their racism, albeit a benign form of the disease; but to those who were its target, the pain was the same as that produced by the crack of a Klansman's whip. Maybe it was worse, because most southern Blacks didn't expect that sort of thing from northerners.

I will never forget the look on a black woman's face when she was pushed out of her chair by a white woman from New York who felt she could type faster and more efficiently. That, and many similar incidents, was evidence to me that racism wasn't really being conquered by the civil rights crusade. True, progress was being made in eliminating two of its symptoms – racial segregation and discrimination – but the disease remained virtually untouched.

We applauded the civil rights legislation pushed through Congress by President Lyndon Johnson. America, many felt, had entered a more progressive phase in its social development. It looked promising. In fact, there was a short period of time – right after the historic legislation was passed – when many Blacks believed that they had finally reached the 'Promised Land', that they were being accepted as equals by their white fellow country-men, and that racism was dead. But they soon discovered that the reality was far less hopeful than what they had expected. They had tried in good faith to integrate and had been rejected.

I never voiced my doubts to my colleagues, or anyone else for that matter. Had I tried, I would have been considered crazy. But what had happened the night after Dr King's assassination was a confirmation that my intuition was correct.

On the day of the assassination I received an urgent phone call from a Teaneck, New Jersey, official. He wanted to know if our guest, Robert Hayden, would be willing to participate in a special memorial service for Dr King the next night. Our town adminis-tration knew that the highly acclaimed poet was in Teaneck because the Bahá'ís had publicized a talk he was to give. Mr Hayden consented to take part in the service.

The high school auditorium was packed. In fact, people were sitting in the aisles and standing at the back, both in the orchestra section and balcony. Prayers were read by different clergymen. A church choir sang. And one dignitary after another proclaimed that Dr King had not died in vain.

Robert Hayden, who was the last speaker, strode to the podium, hunched over it, gripped it tightly with both of his black hands, then peered out at the audience through his thick glasses for about a minute without uttering a word. There was no restlessness in the audience, because everyone sensed that they were about to hear something profound. And they were right.

'Dr Martin Luther King Junior may have died in vain,' the poet declared with deep emotion in his voice, 'because racism is alive; it flows through the arteries of America.'

After a pause to allow what he said to sink in, Robert Hayden recited his poem, 'Frederick Douglass':

When it is finally ours, this freedom, this liberty, this beautiful
and terrible thing, needful to man as air,

usable as earth; when it belongs at last to all,
when it is truly instinct, brain matter, diastole, systole,
reflex action; when it is finally won; when it is more
than the gaudy mumbo jumbo of politicians:
this man, this Douglass, this former slave, this Negro
beaten to his knees, exiled, visioning a world
where none is lonely, none hunted, alien,
this man, superb in love and logic, this man
shall be remembered. Oh, not with statues' rhetoric,
not with legends and poems and wreaths of bronze alone,
but with lives grown out of his life, the lives
fleshing his dream of the beautiful, needful thing.

The audience was taken aback. They hadn't come to hear that. They had assumed that the distinguished man of letters would eulogize Dr King, and perhaps even recite a poem that he had specially written for the occasion. Although the service was over, some men and women remained in their seats for awhile, mulling over Hayden's poem. Deep down these people knew that the poet had told the truth.

I didn't want to applaud, and I didn't feel vindicated. I actually felt sad, sad that there was so much hatred in the land, sad that so many white people refused to recognize that racism was still alive in America, and sad that despite being Robert Hayden's friend, I hadn't been able to free myself from the evil that he, as a black man, had to face every day of his life.

Twenty years have passed since Robert Hayden made that statement in Teaneck, New Jersey. If he were alive today I am sure he would say the same thing. America's racial condition hasn't changed much. Oh, there have been some cosmetic changes, but the basic problem remains the same: the disease is as potent as ever.

The Howard Beach and Forsythe County incidents wouldn't have surprised Robert Hayden; nor would the recent rash of racial violence on university campuses. He knew that the civil rights legislation of the '60s wasn't enough, that in time white folks would find ways of circumventing the laws wherever and whenever possible. For example, private academies have sprung up all over the land; since most Blacks can't afford to send their children to them, the private schools remain white and the public schools become predominantly black. Wealthy and middle class whites have left the larger cities and bought homes in the suburbs. Those whites who can't afford to do this have reinforced their resolve to keep Blacks out of their neighborhoods.

Bussing a few black children into schools in the well-to-do suburbs has proved, in many instances, more disruptive to Blacks than to whites. The inner city youngsters who have had a poorer educational background have been forced to compete with those who have had the benefit of a more privileged education. The clash of cultures has also caused emotional wounds. The black children, a distinct minority, often feel out of place and alienated. Many black parents have withdrawn their children from the bussing program, lest their youngsters become psychologically crippled.

Because most black college students have found it difficult to adjust to life in predominantly white universities, they have tended to band together, creating a social gulf between Black and white on campus. As for those black students who have tried to integrate, many have been forced to abandon their culture and adopt the white man's ways. In the end, they have learned that their sacrifice did not achieve their objective, which was to be completely accepted by the white community. As a result, more and more black young men and women – who are now being sought after by the best white universities – are either attending college at all-black schools or have given up the idea of furthering their education.

13

BY WORKING in New York I got to meet some famous people. Among them were leading equal rights activists, two of whom had a profound impact on me.

I interviewed Dr Martin Luther King several times. I was impressed with him each time we met. To me his magnetism didn't come from what he said, though his words were a powerful source of attraction. He could have been sitting in silence, and I still would have been drawn to him. Each time we met I learned something new about the man. He was always in control, even when reporters fired sticky questions at him. His response was never harsh, never a put-down; he never resorted to sarcasm. His manner didn't change in private. He was consistently sincere. Dr King exuded a strength that had to come from deep faith, a faith fashioned from a lifetime of reflection and prayer. He didn't have to say he believed in God; being with him you just knew he did.

There was no question in my mind that he knew what he had to do and that he had thought deeply about how he was going to do it. While he had his sight fixed on his objectives, he would take the time to respond to those with concerns other than his own. I experienced that while covering one of his trips to New York.

After his speech one evening, I – and about 20 other reporters – rushed to the stage to ask Dr King questions. With microphones thrust in his face, he calmly responded to the newsmen's queries regarding the civil rights movement. Though I was there to ask the same kind of questions, I wanted to bring up an issue only indirectly connected to the American civil rights campaign. I wanted to tell him about the persecution of the Moroccan Bahá'ís.

The practical side of me hesitated – how would I explain such an unorthodox action to my editor? But I saw in Dr King a quality that I admired but hadn't personally developed: he seemed to me like someone you could bare your soul to. And that's what I did, amidst a corps of hard-nosed reporters who were jockeying for position to ask the appropriate questions.

They must have thought I was crazy when I asked Dr King if he had heard about the plight of the Bahá'ís of Morocco. His reaction was what I knew it would be. He moved closer to me, his eyes reflecting deep concern. I don't know how long we stood there talking, oblivious of the press corps, the autograph-seekers and other admirers, black and white. It was as if I wasn't on assignment and we were engaged in a private conversation. He wanted to know the scope of the persecution, and what had precipitated it. He asked what form the persecution had taken, and if anyone had been harmed. When I told him that several Bahá'ís had been sentenced to death for practicing their Faith, he shook his head as if to say, 'When will man's inhumanity to man stop?'

An aide came by, pointing to his watch, but Dr King didn't turn away from me. He continued to listen, and then told me that he knew some Bahá'ís and that he was impressed with the Faith's teachings. Before leaving, he suggested that the Bahá'í leadership take the problem to the United Nations, and then asked what he could do to help relieve the pressure on the Moroccan Bahá'ís.

Through that brief encounter with Dr King, I gained an appreciation of what a human being is capable of attaining spiritually. He wasn't only universal in his thinking; he was universal in his being. While we were together, his attitude freed me from my prejudices. I was lifted into a realm where love dominates, and because of that I was not fearful, or suspicious, or selfish. I was free. The only other time I had felt that way was with the Washingtons and David Penn. Though my friends were Bahá'ís and Dr King was a Christian, they all radiated the same kind of power; they were plugged into the same source. To me, that was a clue as to how I had to deal with my racism.

While I never had a personal conversation with Malcolm X, I covered some of his speeches in auditoriums and on street corners. There were a number of times when I was in a pack of reporters hounding him for a reaction to a story that involved him in some way.

I wish I had had the opportunity to speak to him on a one-to-one basis. I admired him greatly. Years later I read his autobiography and my admiration for him was reinforced.

To me he was an honest man, pure-hearted, not afraid to say and do what was right even if it flew in the face of the stiff organized opposition by both Blacks and whites. He was not an opportunist who tried to gain power and notoriety by exploiting a vulnerable social condition. There was no question in my mind but that he would have been willing to sacrifice his life if it could have freed America's black people. And Blacks living in the ghettos knew that, even those who didn't subscribe to his religious philosophy.

I remember the first time I covered one of his street rallies. This was before he had made his pilgrimage to Mecca where he embraced the principle of the oneness of mankind and decided to devote himself to its promulgation.

It was twilight when a large crowd gathered outside of the Hotel Theresa on 125th Street that hot Saturday in July. While they waited for Malcolm X to arrive, my film crew had already set up a good shooting position. They seemed apprehensive about being in the heart of Harlem as the only whites in the crowd. Five or six boys – they must have been nine or ten years old – were selling the Black Muslim newspaper *Mohammed Speaks*. They sensed the film crew's uneasiness and approached them with their wares. The cameraman, electrician and sound engineer bought a bunch of newspapers from each one of the youngsters. I guess it was their way of buying protection.

I had never covered one of Malcolm X's rallies before, and I felt a bit apprehensive myself. I had heard from others, both whites and Blacks, that he hated white people. I, too, purchased a copy of *Mohammed Speaks*, which I found interesting reading. There were not only articles on black history, but stories about what the Black Muslim movement was doing in the way of social and economic development in the black communities across the nation. I was impressed and wondered why it had not received much press.

When Malcolm X stepped to the microphone, the crowd quieted down. I don't think I have ever heard a man speak with greater conviction and clarity. He didn't read from a prepared text; nor did he use notes. What he said poured from his heart and was carefully refined and channeled by his fine mind. His delivery was polished. While he didn't use big words, he conveyed big concepts; and to most whites they were scary. I can see why many white men and women felt he was a dangerous radical, for no one likes being called a 'white devil'. He used that term more than once at the rally. At first I was taken aback. I felt singled out, as if a prison yard light was being trained on me. The old fear I had during my early days in Chicago surfaced, the fear of being alone in a crowd of angry ghetto Blacks. Though I was extremely self-conscious, no one in the crowd even looked at me. Nor did Malcolm X. I sensed that to him, and to those around him, my TV crew and I didn't exist. They didn't even glance my way when the words 'white devil' boomed out so that all of Harlem could hear.

After awhile the fact that no one noticed me made me feel less anxious, and I got caught up in what Malcolm X was saying. As I listened, I stopped worrying about being in Harlem, outnumbered by Blacks. The term 'white devil' no longer seemed threatening. How had I experienced such a quick change of attitude?

When I was writing up the Malcolm X story, it dawned on me why I had experienced an attitude change. Being exposed to the truth does that to you. What Malcolm X told the crowd was absolutely true. There is such a creature as a 'white devil' – and I was one.

Of course, I didn't actually see myself as an agent of Satan – I had never believed in a personified devil but rather believed that bad behavior is learned. When Malcolm X referred to the 'white devil', I realized he was referring to the racism that has been pressed into the white man's heart. Malcolm X knew it was there, despite protests to the contrary. It seemed the louder the protest, the more convinced he was that he was right. I felt that he believed that the racism of white people was a patent evil: not only had it created the institution of slavery in America and invented Jim Crowism, but even after all of that had been outlawed, it continued to perpetuate the myth of the black man's inferiority. And Malcolm X did his best to demonstrate how that was manifested, how it hurt Blacks, and how devoid of fact and reason racist thinking was.

Wherever he spoke he drew crowds. It fascinated me to observe the people listening to him. He was able to do what no other black leader could. He said publicly what the average Black in the street wanted, but was afraid, to say. Malcolm X was able to cut through the black man's white-influenced view of himself and elevate him to the station of manhood – a position that was rightfully his but was denied him by the empowered. At Malcolm X's rallies men stood tall.

As he spoke I could sense their fears, doubts and anger leaving them, and a surge of pride and hope pouring into them. Pride and hope played no part in their everyday lives for they had to play certain roles in the white man's world. But standing before Malcolm X, or watching him on TV, Blacks could believe that they didn't have to play those roles.

'Yes, you are fully fledged human beings,' he would assure them. The more they heard him speak, the more convinced they became that the white man's view of them was wrong. Dead wrong.

'Respect as human beings,' he once wrote, 'that's what

American black masses want. That's the true problem. The black masses want not to be shrunk from as though they are plague-ridden. They want not to be walled up in slums, in the ghettos, like animals. They want to live in an open, free society where they can walk with their heads up, like men and women.'

Those who broke with the past and embraced his philosophy had the inner strength to shed vices that they had used as a means of escape from a condition they had believed was impossible to change. They walked with dignity.

I marveled at how fast the converts changed their attitudes and behavior: inwardly and outwardly they became more pure, their families became more united, they viewed work as a happy duty. Many became involved in their religious community's business cooperatives. They volunteered their services to help others overcome their addiction to drugs and alcohol. God became central in their lives. Their relationship with Him became more than a Sunday-only experience; it became an everyday affair. They prayed five times a day and lived life as if God was their constant companion.

While many whites viewed Malcolm X as a fanatic, he was, in reality, extremely open-minded. It was his deep convictions and incisive forthrightness which frightened them and warped their perception of him.

He had to be open-minded to have grown spiritually and intellectually in the way he did. After his father had been murdered by whites, Malcolm X rebelled by pursuing a life of crime. He became a pimp, a drug-pusher, a burglar and an extortionist. While in prison he found God through Islam. His conversion turned him to the light of knowledge, and he basked in it, using it to unearth the truth. When he discovered corruption at the highest level of the Black Muslim movement, he embraced orthodox Islam.

Though his experience in Mecca broadened his outlook, he didn't alter his manner of speaking and his forceful approach in dealing with the evils in society. He continued to lambast hypocrisy whenever he was exposed to it.

I remember in particular a talk he gave on the oneness of humankind. He made a prediction which at the time I found difficult to accept.

'The true uniting of the races in America will come about in the South before the North; because the southern white only has his bigotry to overcome, while the northern white must first overcome his delusion that he isn't a racist, and then deal with his racism.'

About 23 years after he made that prediction I met with Tod Ewing and his wife in South Carolina where they had been living with their two daughters for at least four years.

'When will you be returning to the North?' I asked.

'I doubt if we ever will,' he said.

'What do you mean?'

'We find it less hypocritical here.'

'How?'

'The relationship between the races is more genuine.'

'But what about the KKK and all of that?'

'That's blown out of proportion. Down here, when a white overcomes his racism we embrace like long-lost brothers. I have experienced it.'

14

LIVING in Teaneck, I felt closer to the civil rights movement. The local government was more socially progressive than in any other places we had lived. Quite a few residents had taken part in the march on Washington; some had even participated in freedom marches in the South. Others made regular generous financial contributions to various civil rights endeavors.

There was a fairly large black population in Teaneck, mostly middle-class professionals, some of whom were our friends. But they congregated in the eastern part of town while we lived in the west, literally on the other side of the tracks. We bought a house there because that's where we focused our search. At the time we weren't conscious of the fact that we were avoiding the eastern end of town. We were simply following the course charted by our real estate agent. She assured us that she had our best interests at heart.

We were happy with the house we bought, a sturdy colonial for only $20,000. And we were in a neighborhood with the best elementary school in town.

After awhile we recognized the de facto segregation that was being practiced in that most progressive town of northeastern New Jersey. We realized that we had allowed ourselves to be used to perpetuate the discriminatory social pattern. When it dawned on us that all of our black friends in Teaneck in fact lived in a ghetto, we wanted to do something to open up all the neighborhoods to Blacks. Our prayers were answered.

A black family from New York City wanted to buy the house next door to ours; but its owner, an elderly bachelor who was moving to Florida, refused to sell it to them because he didn't want to 'spoil the neighborhood'. He had long-time friends on our street and was afraid of alienating them. When we learned all of this, our family consulted on what we could do to change the man's mind.

Talking to him proved fruitless. So we consulted again. This time we decided on an action I never expected to take in my lifetime.

Walking the picket line with my wife and children in front of our neighbor's house turned out to be one of the proudest moments in my life. Our children ranged in age from twelve to two. With the exception of the baby, they all understood why they were picketing. They were so enthusiastic about what they were doing that they refused to go inside to eat lunch; they ate their sandwiches on the picket line.

Some of the residents in the neighborhood who agreed with our point of view joined us. News of what we were doing spread, and the local weekly newspaper sent a photographer and reporter to the scene. The police patrol wagon came by several times, but never stopped to ask what we were doing. I suspect our neighbor, who refused to come out, called the police, hoping they would put an end to the demonstration.

It didn't take long for the elderly home-owner to change his mind. In a few months the black family moved into the house next door.

While in Teaneck I experienced another human rights victory. Edward Carpenter approached our Local Spiritual Assembly, seeking advice on a critical career matter. As a member of the Assembly, I was struck by Ed's dilemma. He had a secure counseling position at Queens College with all sorts of benefits, and he was being asked to give it up. A group of community leaders wanted him to head a private alternative high school in

Harlem for young men and women who had been branded uneducable by the public school system for alleged behavioral problems. Down deep he wanted to take the job, because he could identify with the youth who would attend the school. He himself had been brought up in Harlem and had had serious problems negotiating the public school system. He therefore felt he could help the so-called school 'drop-outs'.

Ed also wanted the chance to make Harlem Preparatory School a source of pride to a community that had been terribly neglected through the years by the city administration. Harlem had never had a high school in Ed's day, and he remembered traveling long distances by subway and bus to go to school in a different part of the city.

The Assembly consulted on Ed's problem for hours, reviewing the risk he would be taking by accepting the new position: he would be giving up a tenured position for one whose funding was based on philanthropy. However, everyone knew that had Ed not been a family man, there would have been no question but that he would take the job, even though the school was to operate out of an abandoned supermarket and there wasn't enough money to establish an adequate library.

The Assembly advised Ed to take the job because with it he would have the opportunity to free young men and women from the cycle of poverty and despair that they were locked into. The Assembly expressed its faith in his ability to succeed in transforming his vision into something substantial, something that would inspire other communities. With the Assembly's blessing, Ed took the job.

While Harlem Prep gained national prominence, the school's success was hammered out on the anvil of pain. During difficult times – and there were many – Ed would bring his problems to the Assembly. One incident in particular stands out.

A certain militant element seized the school because it wanted its particular black power philosophy to be taught. It was opposed to Ed's insistence that racial unity be promoted. He had opened the school to whites and Puerto Ricans as well as Blacks –

all school drop-outs. Ed had also put together an integrated faculty. He strongly felt that one way of overcoming racism was to foster racial unity, to teach and live the principle of the oneness of humankind.

The black power group was deadly serious. They not only occupied the school building, they also threatened Ed's life. And he was very much aware of their reputation for carrying out whatever they promised to do.

Ed appealed to the Assembly for guidance. It was a sensitive matter. Asking help from the police would alienate certain community groups who trusted Ed but were anti-establishment. Another approach was needed, and the Assembly produced one that worked.

Following the Assembly's advice, Ed organized a group made up of many different factions to publicly demonstrate their support for him and his school. This group made it known that any obstruction to Ed's program would cause the children – already neglected by the public school system – to continue to suffer.

The men who seized the school got the message. They not only walked out of the building, some of them walked back in as students. And Ed welcomed them with open arms.

As a consultant to Harlem Prep I witnessed how that miracle of an educational institution operated. One day, for example, three students approached Ed and asked if they could produce a film on fascism. He was impressed with their enthusiasm, but he knew that they lacked the basic skills to carry out their proposed project.

'You could do it,' he said, 'but you first have to write a script, and the information for the script is in books.'

The three squirmed at the mention of books. They had been brought up to believe that the book was 'the white man's thing'. They saw books as a symbol of their oppression.

The students produced the film, but not before they had pored over history, political science and economics books. They worked with their English and communications teachers in drafting a script. It was an agonizing process, much like giving birth. There was pain, lots of pain, but the result was rewarding. Making the film was a real-life undertaking in which the school provided the resources that could be tapped to make the project successful. Those students seemed to have learned more doing that project than in all the time they had spent in other schools.

I could understand why Ed looked forward to the graduation exercises. I sensed what he and the local residents must have felt when the graduating class was introduced to the crowd and the students received their diplomas. The crowd was witnessing a miracle: black men and women were heading for some of the best universities and colleges in America.

One year I participated in the graduation ceremonies, and I'll never forget it. It was a sunny, warm June morning. Thousands of people, the honored guests and neighborhood onlookers, were gathered around the makeshift stage, which extended from the east wall of the Hotel Theresa, the same spot where some of Malcolm X's rallies were held. Ed, the faculty, and the graduating class were on the stage. I was in the audience, in the front row, with all of the people being honored that day. I was swept up by the bright spirit of rebirth that permeated the atmosphere. It was a triumphant time, not just because a group of Harlem students were graduating from high school, but because they were winning a freedom that had been denied them for so long. Every time I looked at the graduates I cried.

Pride was etched on the faces of the onlookers, those in the crowds and those peering down from their open tenement windows and fire escapes. They broke into applause time and time again for no apparent reason. I knew that their clapping was something deeper than mere appreciation. It was a response that springs from a joyful soul, an outpouring of love, an expression of deliverance. Even the black policemen who were rerouting traffic were moved by the proceedings. Whenever they glanced over to the stage I sensed pride welling up in them.

As I drank in the spirit of this unusual celebration, I thought of Teaneck's Local Spiritual Assembly. Had it not been for the

Assembly, I thought, the chances are that all of this would have never happened.

The graduation ceremony was one of the highlights of my life: I witnessed young men and women finding hope, something that they had learned early in life didn't exist for them; I witnessed a man's dream, which many considered a fantasy, come into being; and I witnessed a Bahá'í Spiritual Assembly providing the kind of guidance and encouragement that a community needs in order to free itself from social patterns that squelch the human spirit and perpetuate social decay.

I was so moved by the experience that when I returned home that day I dashed upstairs to my typewriter and wrote an essay on how to achieve racial unity in America. I felt I was guided because there was such a rush of ideas that came to me. I felt that what I was writing had to be written. I was sure it was an important piece. When Carol – probably my toughest critic – said she liked it, I knew it wasn't merely a series of powerfully-phrased sentences which were really only a vehicle for pent-up emotions.

I was sure that every black person would love my essay, so I shared it with the first one I saw. It was three days after the graduation ceremony. Oscar was a Bahá'í who had stopped by to drop off a report he had prepared for the Assembly. It didn't matter to me that it was supper time; I just had to have him hear what I had written.

With deep feeling and exuberance, I read for 20 minutes, never looking up once. When I finished, I expected Oscar to clap, to shout 'Bravo', to express some form of enthusiasm. But there was no response. He sat on the edge of the sofa not because he was enthralled by what I had written, but because he wanted to leave. I searched his face for some sign of approval. I wanted to ask him what he thought of the essay, but I was afraid to. It was obvious that he was upset, and I wasn't inclined to find out why.

Oscar stood up and said, 'My mother is expecting me for supper, so I better get going.'

'Oh, I see,' I said.

'I'll see you at the Assembly meeting on Wednesday.'

'That's right!' I said, feeling cheated that I hadn't had an enthusiastic response to my essay.

It was difficult to accept Oscar's apparent rejection of something I believed in so much. At first I thought that perhaps he lacked the depth to appreciate what I had written. Maybe his vision had been blurred by the suffering he had had to endure as an American Black. I was puzzled, because I was sure he couldn't argue with the essay's content, a view as to how both races could unite. It was something I knew he wanted to see happen; and the essay was based on the Bahá'í teachings, which he accepted.

Was it the tone of my voice? Or the manner in which I presented myself? I didn't sleep much that night. The warm milk didn't help, nor did the deep-breathing exercises Carol used whenever she had trouble sleeping. Eventually I went to my study and sat in the dark wondering why Oscar had reacted in such a way.

I wanted to know in the worst way what Oscar really thought of the essay. For without his evaluation I was hesitant to share it with others. If I had written something that was offensive, I wanted to know what it was, so that I could correct it.

I turned the light on and re-read the essay probably ten times, trying to determine what he may have found offensive.

I was convinced that there was absolutely nothing which I had written that Oscar could disagree with. And I knew him very well. As Bahá'ís we shared the same religious beliefs, and for five years we served on the same Assembly together. We also knew each other's background. But when I said to myself, 'and we are friends', I realized that he might not consider me his friend. Friendship is based on mutual respect, on shared feelings, on having fun together.

'Do I respect Oscar?' I asked myself. 'Do I feel he's my equal?'

I couldn't give an unqualified 'Yes'. I knew that we had never shared personal feelings with one another; neither of us had ever confided in the other. We had never been to a concert together, or a ball game or a movie. In reality, Oscar was a religious associate of mine, not a friend. I never talked to him about things he was interested in other than religion and topics associated with it. I never invited him over for dinner; nor did I ever eat at his house. The same was true with all of the other black Bahá'ís in town. The only socializing we did was during the Bahá'í meetings. When I thought about it, I didn't have one real friend in New Jersey who was black, although I had always considered all of the Blacks I knew in the eastern end of Teaneck as my friends.

I began to see how Oscar might have felt used when I virtually forced him to hear my essay on race. I was looking for a black response to what I had written. I wasn't interested in what Oscar the human being thought of my ideas. While he probably resented my ignoring his individuality, he must also have resented always having to talk about racial matters when he was with whites. He was no expert on the subject other than from his experiences as a Black living and working in a white-dominated society.

Frankly, Oscar was tired of talking about racism with whites and then having to live and work in a white society. It accentuated the differences between Blacks and whites. Because of that, Oscar was unable to establish a natural bond with a white person. When with whites, he felt more like a symbol than a human being.

I THOUGHT I would never leave NBC. But I did leave and for a job for which I had no training – teaching at a university. Only Dr Dwight Allen, the flamboyant and innovative Dean of the University of Massachusetts School of Education would think of hiring someone without a graduate degree to head an academic department, with all of the rights and privileges that entails.

Among my concerns about moving to Amherst was that there seemed little opportunity to associate with people of color. At first glance it seemed like such a homogeneous place. But I was wrong. Soon after we moved to the quaint New England town I began to act as faculty advisor to *Drum*, the black literary magazine on campus. I held the post all the time I taught there, working with four different editors.

I never found out why I was chosen for that particular job. I was curious, of course, particularly because the University had a number of black professors, most of them connected with the department of Afro-American Studies. My guess is that I was chosen because the four editors I worked with were Bahá'ís.

Of all the religious groups at Amherst, the Bahá'ís were the most racially diverse. Blacks from the South, Midwest, California and Africa were drawn to the University of Massachusetts largely because of the Dean of the School of Education, both a Bahá'í and one of the most innovative educators in the land. There were also

East Indians, Persians, Hispanics, Japanese, and people of Jewish background. Because of the rich diversity in the Bahá'í community, I found attending Bahá'í meetings an exhilarating experience. It was especially rewarding for our children.

While most people on campus were impressed with the unusual racial composition of the Bahá'í community, there were some who resented it. A few black professors and staff members were extremely upset by the number of black students – graduate and undergraduate – who became Bahá'ís, students like the four *Drum* editors. One professor, when he learned that the chairman of the university's Afro-American organization, Robert Henderson, was a Bahá'í, publicly stated, 'They are taking the cream of the crop!'

To stop what they felt was the erosion of the black community on campus, some of the professors started rumors designed to discredit the Dean and the Bahá'í Faith. One rumor had it that Dr Allen's father owned a pineapple plantation in Africa and that the workers were treated as slaves.

The opposition grew uglier. The threat of physical injury was employed to persuade those Blacks who had joined the Bahá'í Faith to drop out. The threats couldn't be taken lightly. For awhile the young black Bahá'ís didn't walk alone on campus – they walked in pairs, and they made sure that one of them was big and strong.

The Bahá'í community was shaken by this apparent attack on the Faith. It wasn't particularly recruiting young black men and women, or anyone else, for that matter. Nor did it wish the dissolution of the black community on campus. No one was coerced into joining the Bahá'í Faith. The students joined because they wanted to join. They had been moved by the genuine interracial harmony in the Amherst Bahá'í community. That, more than anything else, sparked their sincere inquiry into the Faith. One student had been a member of the Black Panthers, perhaps the most militant Black-power group in America at the time. Prior to his meeting with the Bahá'ís he had felt that it was impossible for the races to unite. He tested the Bahá'ís – at times severely – before joining.

It was difficult for me to understand why Blacks, most of them learned men and women, were attacking a group that was sincerely promoting racial unity; there were probably more racially mixed married couples among the Bahá'ís than in any other group its size in the Amherst area.

After some probing, I discovered the major reason. Most of the professors and staff members feared that some force within the white establishment was using the Bahá'ís to divide the black movement on campus. Without unity, they felt, they were powerless to change the racist conditions on campus.

Eventually we were able to assure the black leadership of our motives, and the attacks subsided, though there were still a few jabs at us from time to time.

To Dwight Allen's credit, he didn't allow the attacks on him to dissuade him from organizing a crusade by the School of Education dedicated to wiping out institutionalized racial prejudice in schools throughout Massachusetts. Most of the professors whom he had personally recruited enthusiastically endorsed the idea. A spirit of invincibility was whipped up at faculty meetings. We really believed that our crusade was going to achieve its goals. Some of us couldn't wait for its launching. We called ourselves 'social change agents', an early-1970s synonym for reformer.

To create a strategy, the Dean organized a retreat on Nantucket Island. The majority of the faculty and staff showed up. It was an exciting experience for we felt that what we were about to launch was an historic program. If it succeeded – and we had no doubt of its success – we would have created a model for other schools of education throughout the nation to emulate.

When Dean Allen announced the launch of the project on campus, there was some snickering in the audience, especially among the faculty members who weren't participating in the program. We soon found out there were many other skeptics, black and white, both at the university and in the town. We even received some criticism from Boston, the state capital. But we were undaunted – with Dwight Allen leading the charge.

After only one semester the complexion of the School of

Education grew darker. One Black was named an associate Dean; another, an assistant Dean. Several other Blacks were hired, one of them being made head of one of the School's most successful programs. More black graduate students were recruited. We didn't have to recruit very hard because news of the crusade reached black communities across the country. Of the seven doctoral candidates that were accepted in my program, four of them were Blacks, including Ed Carpenter.

The School of Education stood out on campus as an academic oasis of racial diversity. Because the news media made a big thing of it, as well as of the school's innovative programs, the School of Education emerged swiftly from its reputation as a sleepy, conservative center of higher learning into a serious competitor of the Education departments of Harvard and Stanford Universities, the perennial leaders in the educational field.

Despite the progress that was made within the School, few changes were achieved outside of the University, leaving people like me frustrated and angry.

Why did the crusade fail? I feel there were a number of reasons. Of course, with the passage of time we are able to make a sharper assessment of the project.

There were some people on campus, both black and white, who were bent on derailing the crusade. Some academic purists, for example, felt strongly that a university should not become a force for social change, that its primary mandate was to educate students in academic subjects. Then there were the few black professors who resented having a white person conceive and spearhead a crusade to free Blacks. Somehow, they saw the crusade as a reflection on their manhood, that they lacked the strength to fight their own battles. But what irritated most of the opponents was the Dean's approach. His public pronouncement that it was his being a Bahá'í which motivated him to launch the crusade upset a wide cross-section of people on campus.

The Dean's enemies in the School of Education pounced, charging him with using the crusade to promote his religion. Of course, those of us who knew Dwight well, knew that that was

107

not the case: Dwight was simply being honest. As a Bahá'í he was committed to combatting racism and working for racial unity. To him he was doing what was natural.

Because the Faith was being attacked, the Amherst Spiritual Assembly decided to look into the problem. After a hurried but complete investigation into all the facts, which necessitated long consultations for seven days in a row, the Assembly concluded that public mention of the Faith by Bahá'í employees at the University should be curtailed temporarily.

Dwight asked for a hearing and was granted one. But his appeal against the Assembly's decision was turned down. He then appealed to the Bahá'í National Spiritual Assembly, of which he was a member that year. After its review, the National Assembly unanimously upheld the Amherst Assembly's decision: Dwight had voted against his own appeal.

While the informal anti-crusade and pro-crusade debate raged on campus, unrest was developing among many black students at the School of Education. They felt that changes weren't happening fast enough, that the appointment of black deans and faculty members and the enrolling of more black and Hispanic students were only cosmetic. What needed changing, they felt, was the School's soul, which they claimed was racist. When white professors, many of them passionate supporters of the crusade, vigorously defended the School, many of the black students rebelled, helped by a few black professors. A revolution erupted, with the rebellious students seizing the School and holding Dean Allen hostage for several days.

When the rebels felt that their case had been made and heard, they released Dean Allen and removed the barricades. Another factor in ending the rebellion was their fear that they might seriously hinder their chances of earning an advanced degree, which, they felt, would help them gain greater influence in the political system.

Why would students, who were being helped by Dean Allen, turn on him? At the time I was too close to the situation to be able to assess it clearly. But later, and after consulting with those, both black and white, who had been involved, I felt I could answer the question. It had a lot to do with my own particular problem with racism.

Many of the black students had been easily exploitable. To a large degree, they had developed a love-hate relationship with the Dean. They felt that in theory the concept of the crusade was good. Deep down they wanted it to achieve its goals, but they had serious doubts that it would. Their doubts were based on feelings they found difficult to explain to a white person, for they believed that only someone who has experienced the humiliation, the pain and frustration a black person faces daily would understand. They were right, too, because when they expressed their doubts, white professors became terribly defensive. To the rebelling black students that reaction confirmed their doubts. They viewed the Dean's accomplishment of altering the School's social composition a good first step, and the installation of socially-sensitive academic programs as a good second step; but the students felt that more steps were necessary – many more. For while many whites applauded what the School of Education had achieved, many black students looked upon the advancements as the lengthening of the chain of racism that was securely fastened to their necks and firmly anchored in America's heart. With the changes at the School of Education, the black students could see and do things that had been denied them in the past, but there were still limitations, and when they tried to enter forbidden areas, they were jerked back into place. What the students wanted the School of Education, the University, the state, the whole nation to know was that they wanted the chain severed forever.

I think that the Dean heard the black students' cry, and wanted to do what the students demanded, but he knew that only a change of heart on the part of the whites would truly alter the situation. It wasn't enough to espouse liberal principles, to belong to progressive societies and to be involved in peace and human rights causes. What was most important was to recognize one's own racism and to work actively to rid oneself of it. I think those

Blacks who became Bahá'ís saw in the Bahá'í community both a genuine effort to do that and a fellowship that was real. Maybe Dwight Allen's mention of the Bahá'í Faith in his public addresses at the University was a desperate appeal for Blacks and whites on campus to look into what he knew in his heart was a way of truly eliminating racism in America.

16

FROM the School of Education experience I learned that even a fairly large group of PhDs who know how destructive racism is, and who are dedicated to wiping it out, won't be able to achieve their objectives unless they first free themselves of the thing they are trying to overcome in others. One of the major stumbling blocks to the eradication of racism in America is the difficulty of convincing those who claim they aren't racially prejudiced that they are, and that they ought to do something about it.

It is so easy to fool ourselves on the racism issue. I think how enthusiastic we had been about our crusade. We were intoxicated by the thought of victory, of winning the big game. Because of our expertise in dealing with social issues, we believed that we could succeed where others had tried and failed. So many attempts had been made in the past, so many battles had been fought: the abolitionist movement, the Civil War in which 620,000 men died, the race riots, the civil rights movement of the 1960s, Affirmative Action, school bussing, the federal, state and city anti-discrimination legislation. All of that had not loosened the stranglehold of racism on the heart of America.

Why, I wondered, is racism so firmly entrenched in my country? I had discovered how I had become infected, but how had my parents, my sister and brother become infected? I knew they had unwittingly bought into it because they wanted to fit into American society; but what had spawned the disease in the first place, a disease that took on more than epidemic proportions, that seemed to resist all attempted cures, and which had evolved into an acceptable aspect of our culture?

To find out how this spirit-crippling disease had taken hold of a nation that claims to be the most free in the world, I felt I had to explore the past. I couldn't use the history textbooks I had studied in college; they were mostly an elaboration of the propaganda I had been exposed to in the fifth and sixth grades. Like Pete, I remembered the sort of pictures of Blacks that graced our books. By omitting the story of what people of African descent had done for our country, and the story of how they had managed to survive, students of history were led to believe that American Blacks constituted, as a group, a sub-class of the national population.

Racism is more than racial prejudice. When institutionalized, it reflects a national attitude. It is a force that can infiltrate every aspect of a nation. It is so all-encompassing, so much a part of the normal pattern of life that it is difficult for the white person to detect anything other than the most flagrant outbursts of bigotry. I'm sure the college I attended in Indiana never considered itself a racist institution, yet it prohibited the entry of black women students as late as the 1950s and admitted only five or six black men annually. Unlike a personal prejudice such as a dislike of the color blue, or skinny people, or cats, institutionalized racism is a collective prejudice shared by the great majority of a national community.

In the past, racism was expressed openly, but in our socially enlightened era, many whites are more clever at concealing it from themselves; however, they can't hide it from most Blacks, who have been sensitized to spot it. In addition, many Blacks aren't aware of the effect racism has had on them. The indoctrination has been so complete that they often accept the prevailing white man's view of themselves. Simply put, Blacks harbor a subconscious sense of inferiority, while most whites harbor an inherent sense of superiority.

Many Blacks still try to become more like whites. An unofficial status structure has been established, with the lighter skinned men and women being envied by the darker skinned. Certain black college fraternities and sororities discriminate against darker skinned students. For example, one sorority has a rule that applicants for membership mustn't be darker than a tan shopping bag; another one won't allow a woman to join if the veins in her hands don't have the bluish cast that white hands have. There are Blacks who try to conceal their thick lips. Sadly, racism has ingrained in Blacks a self-hatred. While there is a serious effort to overcome that attitude in the black community today, progress is very slow; what is impressed into a people over many generations isn't easily eradicated.

Perhaps one of the greatest agonies one can endure is the knowledge that you have been brainwashed. Like Pete, who felt nervous when he saw a Black driving the subway train he was on, many whites would worry about their safety if they knew that a Black was the pilot of the plane they were on. No wonder airline ads only feature whites as pilots and engineers and Blacks as stewards, clerks and baggage handlers. It is to assure the viewer, both black and white, that only the most trustworthy, brightest and most experienced people fly their planes. Featuring black pilots would trigger a sense of insecurity in the audience. Why? Because we feel that Blacks are inferior to whites. We don't expect Blacks to hold truly responsible positions. The fact that one or two have become astronauts is seen as a gesture to placate civil rights agitators and to create the impression that all of the government's agencies are integrated. We seriously doubt that a black person could do what John Glenn did.

It is like what happened to a black friend of mine who arrived early at a college lecture hall to review her notes before giving her talk. A white woman, a noted human rights activist, approached my friend and asked when the speaker was expected. When the black woman told the inquirer that she was the lecturer, the white woman was surprised. She had been conditioned to seeing Blacks only as janitors, messengers or porters, not as professionals. Her reaction sprang from a basic feeling she had about Blacks, a feeling which her sense of morality kept her from recognizing.

It was something I was personally familiar with. I remember an incident that took place a number of years ago, after a Bahá'í meeting in my home. I couldn't find my wallet. I thought I had left it on the dressing bureau in our bedroom. When I discovered it was missing, the first thing that came to mind was the two black young men who attended the meeting. Somehow, I thought, one of them had taken it on his way to the bathroom. The light in the bedroom had been left on. I was actually angry at those men, but wouldn't dare confront them for fear of being seen as a racist. A couple of hours later I found the wallet, with all of the cash and credit cards intact, on the bathroom sink where I had apparently left it. I realized then that my racism was still a reality. Those ugly thoughts had surfaced, thoughts that I didn't want associated with me. But those thoughts which festered in the remote corridors of my mind were part of me. That was the horrible truth!

Through my personal struggle, I believe I have been able to uncover what led to the development of our national racial attitude, which causes in us that deep negative feeling, that feeling we are ashamed of when it surfaces. We know it is a psychological cancer but we seem helpless in treating it. The deeply-entrenched attitude that pervades every aspect of our national life isn't a recent phenomenon. It didn't result from an untimely twist of nature, nor from an accident. Greed, unadulterated greed, put into motion a carefully crafted premise about the nature of black people. Over the years the premise has been supported by pseudo-scientific findings and philosophical pronouncements by highly respected thinkers. The contention was that Blacks were merely pagan savages, not fully human.

In order to support this view, care was taken to ignore the rich heritage of the Blacks. They are descendants of people who lived in highly advanced civilizations. They were producing iron when the Europeans were still in the Stone Age. The Kingdom of Ghana, which flourished from the sixth to the eleventh centuries, maintained large towns with skillfully-designed buildings. The people of Ghana engaged in elaborate sculpture and metalwork and were prosperous in commerce. Their trading contacts reached as far as Baghdad and Cairo. A complex political structure governed the kingdom, sporting an army of 200,000 men. The Kingdom of Mali produced another outstanding culture. Southern Europeans traveled to Timbuktu, Mali's capital, to study with the local scholars. There was a deep belief in God in both Kingdoms, and prayer was a common practice. The people whom the Europeans were enslaving were neither savages nor pagans.

It didn't take long before the distorted view of Blacks evolved into a belief so deeply ingrained in both Black and white that it is difficult to extricate from the hearts of the adults of this generation. So much a part of the American culture did it become that I probably breathed it in with my first breath.

It was greed that spawned racism. Racism is an outgrowth of the highly profitable industry of slavery. Slavery of black Africans was first developed as an international industry by Europeans. Later, New England traders and Southern plantation-owners – most of them church-going, God-fearing men – extended the practice.

When Pope Nicholas V in 1452 sanctioned the enslavement of the 'African pagans' as a means of Christianizing them, many slave traders felt that their endeavors were divinely blessed. For the next 200 years the Papacy voiced no opposition to slavery. In fact, the Vatican cooperated with those nations engaged in slave trade. In the 1600s the colonial Puritan church in the New World gave its blessing to the slave enterprise as well.

The church's position was based on Biblical passages which were interpreted to uphold the idea that black people were sinners. Influential churchmen used the pulpit to put forward this view with powerful conviction. Many of them, of course, had financial connections with the slave traders. Pressed into the minds of those in the pews was the Book of Genesis and its image of the sinner Ham, who was black and cursed and destined to be 'a hewer of wood'. St Paul's views of the servant's obligation to his master were also emphasized. A leading Puritan cleric, Increase Mather, once thundered from his pulpit, 'You that are servants, you have been guilty of stubborn disobedient carriage toward your masters, though God in His word tells you that you ought to be obedient to them with fear and trembling.'

Reinforcing the growing belief that Blacks were a sub-human species were the views of philosopher John Locke, considered both in England and in the New World as the leading champion of the age of liberal enlightenment. His concept of natural rights was embodied in the Declaration of Independence. Many of the great early Americans like Thomas Jefferson were influenced by Locke's thinking. Locke believed that democracy was for the whites and slavery for the Blacks. So the call of the Declaration of Independence for the establishment of a society where all citizens are equal did not pertain to Blacks.

In all of the original 13 colonies there was the prevailing belief among whites that the Caucasian race was not only superior to the Black race, but that Blacks were part of a lower species, something between the ape and the human. This view was reflected in the drafting of the American Constitution in 1787 when it was declared that a slave was three-fifths of a human being.

With that view inscribed in the most sacred document of the young republic, wealthy northern merchants and southern plantation-owners could argue that slavery was not in conflict with the professed ideals of the American revolution. Slaves, they claimed, were property much like cattle, sheep or pigs. While there were a few small groups like the Quakers who called for the abolition of slavery, their petitions were either summarily rejected or ignored. The dominant view in white America was that Blacks were animals, devoid of human reactions and emotions. With that understanding, the slave owner had no qualms about breaking up a black family, selling the father to a white man in Kentucky, a daughter to a plantation in Maryland, a son to a mill operator in Alabama and keeping the wife and mother, who was sometimes forced into being the master's secret mistress. Killing a black man wasn't considered murder; it was likened to butchering a steer.

This attitude didn't disappear as the nation matured. On the contrary, it was reinforced. The American economy, in large measure, was dependent on slavery. The burgeoning textile industry in New England relied on the cotton planted and picked by slaves in the South. With the invention of the cotton gin, cotton and textile production soared. Because both northern merchants and southern plantation-owners feared that the abolition of slavery would cause their economic demise, they became fierce advocates of the prevailing notion that Blacks were sub-human, citing the three-fifths clause in the Constitution to prove their point. They actively promoted that view in speeches, books and articles. Perhaps the most articulate and persuasive spokesman was the South Carolina senator John C. Calhoun whose powerful intellect and oratory swayed many minds. Many American politicians of the time embraced Calhoun's rationale that slavery was one of the best ways to maintain equality and unity among whites, something that was essential to preserving national solidarity. Calhoun exploited the poor white man's hope of improving his quality of life and his fear of losing whatever status he already had. Calhoun proclaimed that every poor white had the potential of bettering his lot, even growing rich, and that he remained ahead of the Black on America's ladder to success. To preserve his status, the poor white became an advocate of slavery and a firm believer in the inherent inferiority of the Black.

Fueling the prevailing white view of Blacks were the findings of the so-called scientific studies of slaves. Based on the theory that the size of one's head determines creativity and intellectual capacity, scientists such as Dr Josiah C. Nott concluded that Blacks were little above the level of apes. The French philosopher, Count de Gobineau, endorsed this view. His book, *The Inequality of the Human Race*, was published in Philadelphia and circulated among American intellectuals. The Frenchman claimed:

Some of his [the Black's] senses have an acuteness unknown to the

117

other races, the sense of taste and that of smell, for instance . . . But it is precisely this development of the animal faculties that stamps the Negro with the mark of inferiority.

This kind of thinking was popularized by magazines like the *Texas Almanac*. In 1857 it featured an article stating:

. . . the African is an inferior being, differently organized from the white man, with wool instead of hair on his head – with lungs, feet, joints, lips, nose and cranium so distinct as to indicate a different and inferior grade of being.

White supremacists in the North and South welcomed the views of English philosopher Herbert Spencer who was a leading exponent of Darwin's theory of the survival of the fittest. Measured against the white and yellow races, the black man was least fit, he claimed. Much of Spencer's evidence was based on a comparison of the black person's slave condition in America with the white person's free condition. His thesis was that if the Black was truly the equal of the white, he wouldn't have allowed himself to be dominated by the white man.

America's view of Blacks just prior to the Civil War was summed up in the US Supreme Court's Dred Scott decision. Chief Justice Roger Taney declared that Blacks 'are not included, and were not intended to be included, in the word "citizen" in the Constitution . . . being a subordinate and inferior class of beings.'

Abolitionists, meanwhile, clamored for an end to slavery. While their appeals were passionate, and many of them sacrificed much for their cause, their cry didn't change the average white person's basic opinion of the Black. Most white Americans viewed the abolitionists as wild-eyed radicals. Even President Abraham Lincoln's signing of the Emancipation Proclamation had little impact on the prevailing view of Blacks. He himself believed the black race to be inferior to the white.

After the Civil War most whites showed little compassion for the four million freed slaves who had been set loose to live in a world they had not been prepared for. Whites in both the North and the South quickly came to the conclusion that their fundamental feelings about Blacks were justified when they saw the ex-slaves awkwardly trying to adapt to the white man's world. It gave whites cause to believe that Blacks were incapable of living in a civilized society.

The passage by Congress of the Fourteenth Amendment to the Constitution, which eliminated the 'three-fifths' clause, failed to uproot it, however, from the hearts of most whites. The pattern of racial thinking had been set.

America's bloodiest war hadn't really freed the black people; it had simply lengthened the chain. What happened after the Civil War was proof of that. Despite a sincere effort on the part of some northern liberal churchmen to prepare the ex-slaves for life in a free society (the schooling was always in segregated conditions), two kinds of Americans emerged: white people still harboring the strong feeling that Blacks are inherently inferior to whites, and a mass of alienated, frustrated and restricted African-Americans.

About ten years after the war northerners who were once sympathetic to the Blacks' plight turned their attention to other causes. Swept up by the spirit of 'rugged individualism' as exemplified by John D. Rockefeller and J. P. Morgan, they sought to create their own fortunes. Many headed west, ignoring the atrocities being heaped upon Blacks in the South.

Even the White House and Congress turned their backs on what was happening to the ex-slaves. Secret organizations such as the Ku Klux Klan terrorized those Blacks who dared to exercise their rights as citizens. The few whites who sided with the Blacks' cause also came under attack. The Confederacy was reborn in the South, with 'Jim Crowism' replacing slavery. The thousands of Blacks who migrated to the North fared little better than those who remained back home. In both the North and the South Blacks were put in their place – which was far from the advantages enjoyed by whites, but close enough to see what they were being deprived of.

Racism will never be eliminated in America until its citizens overcome their deep-seated belief that Blacks are inherently inferior to whites. Simply put, it is a matter of accepting Blacks as fully fledged human beings. While many whites claim they already do, their behavior usually doesn't reflect what they say.

For example, when US forces invaded Italy in 1943, their commanders had signs placed in the local villages and cities to discourage the mixing of black troops with Italian men and women. The signs declared that black Americans have tails. Even in high places the attitude still exists. A black FBI agent attached to the Omaha office in 1987 learned what many of his fellow agents really thought of him: when he went to his desk one day, he saw that the picture of his family had been cropped and a picture of a monkey's face had been pasted on the body of his son. That same year, the attitude that Blacks are less than human was expressed dramatically in Memphis, Tennessee.

At dawn one day, police were summoned to a black housing project. A young man, who was obviously emotionally upset, was cutting himself with a knife as his mother cried nearby. When the four officers ordered him to drop his knife, he stood up. A policeman reacted by firing two bullets into the young man. Since he was still standing, another volley was fired. This time the young man fell to the ground, still clutching his knife and flailing about. Several more shots quieted him, though he was still moving. According to one eye-witness, a policewoman bent over the bleeding man, pointed her pistol to his head, said, 'Now he won't move anymore,' and fired two more shots.

17

THE solution to my problem came in an unexpected way. While there was no question about my desire to find a solution, the way it came about surprised me. It defied logic. I didn't even have to make a concerted effort to rid myself of what I felt was causing my problem. In fact, had I pursued my original tack I would have still been spinning about frantically, growing more and more agitated. Obtaining what I wanted was simply a case of switching my focus and channeling my energy in another direction. Once I had found the right route, I made up my mind not to look back.

There had been clues along the way: the way I felt in the presence of people like Bessie and George Washington, David Penn, and Dr Martin Luther King. They lifted me into an indescribable state of exaltation. Those extraordinary human beings had one fundamental thing in common – they were spiritually focused. While they were perfectly aware of what was going on around them – and a lot of it was really ugly stuff – they didn't allow it to obscure their vision or impede their resolve to do what had to be done. While they walked the tortuous, unlit highway of life that many of us feel is a chartless way to the grave, their connection to the Divine Source made them glow, allowing them to see things along the way that most of us never notice. Focusing on their light elevated my thoughts to a realm where racism doesn't exist.

But that precious feeling was a burst of inspiration that vanished shortly after those rare individuals were out of sight. Perhaps had I stayed with them longer, I would have realized much sooner that the solution to my problem was spiritual in nature. It was not until I heard a talk given jointly by my son Dale and Karen Streets, a black woman and mutual friend, that I gained some insight as to where the solution was to be found.

They had been invited by the Amherst Bahá'í Community to address what Bahá'ís call 'the most challenging issue' – developing racial unity in America. Much of their talk was based on the teachings of Bahá'u'lláh. It was material I had heard and read before, often at Bahá'í study classes, where I had effectively hidden my problem. But I had failed to grasp the depth of meaning that Dale and Karen had gained from the same passages. I suppose I was so busy pretending to the others that I didn't have a problem that I gave the impression that the Bahá'í teachings condemning racism were really for someone else. In my mind, I turned the study class into an academic exercise, never allowing those precious words to penetrate my heart.

Dale and Karen's talk inspired me to seriously try to relate the Bahá'í teachings and prayers on racial unity to the solving of my problem. Oh, there had been a few times when under extreme pressure I reached for the Bahá'í Writings to resolve a personal racial issue, but I hadn't internalized them. They were something I could talk about at meetings but couldn't apply in everyday life. To me, they were like life-jackets – to be used only when the ship was sinking. The importance of internalizing those teachings struck me as Dale and Karen meticulously went over passages such as this from the Bahá'í Writings:

> The ceaseless exertions which this issue of paramount importance [racism] calls for, the sacrifices it must impose, the care and vigilance it demands, the moral courage and fortitude it requires, the tact and sympathy it necessitates, invest this problem, which the American believers are still far from having satisfactorily resolved, with an urgency and importance that can not be over-estimated.

122

The words 'ceaseless exertions' made me stop and think. While I had been aware of my problem for years, I had found ways to avoid dealing with it. I would grasp onto any available excuse to do something else. Fortunately, through a series of tests, I was forced to deal with it from time to time. I knew that those tests, which could be awfully painful, would continue if I didn't make a sustained effort to overcome my racism. Yet there was also a fear that I would slip further and further away from curing myself of the disease. That, I swore, would never happen again. I wouldn't allow it to happen, because I knew now that overcoming racism was of 'paramount importance', that avoiding the issue would be tantamount to my being unfaithful as a Bahá'í.

I decided to pray every day for help. At first, that's all I could think of doing. Little did I know at the time that my decision to do that was the best decision I could make. Without prayer I could accomplish very little. It wasn't only a daily reminder of what I must do; it was also a means of gaining guidance from God as to how I was going to heed the Bahá'í challenge that 'a revolutionary change in the concept and attitude of the average white American toward his Negro fellow citizen' must take place before racism can be eradicated.

That was a big order. 'A revolutionary change'! Heeding this call meant more than developing a tolerant attitude. It meant uprooting that deep, deep feeling that I had tried hard over the years to tear loose of, and never could. It had become such a frustrating experience that during my weaker moments I used to wonder if it was actually possible to rid myself of that unwanted feeling that Blacks are inherently inferior to whites. Maybe I would have to settle for a purely rational acceptance of the equality of the races and let that suffice. I would just have to do my best to keep the disease from flaring up. But deep down I knew that wasn't possible because in the past I had tried and failed. Something always happened that I couldn't foresee, triggering an eruption.

My reaction to the challenge was to pray harder. That was the only thing I could do; nothing else came to mind. There were no revelations, no instantaneous cures. It was clear that the answer to my prayers was to pray even harder. For an action-oriented person like myself, that was hard to take. Praying harder meant complete concentration, having to beseech God with all my heart and soul for His help – even crying for His help. Prayer was an acknowledgment of my helplessness; it was a surrendering of my will to God's. I had tried to solve my problem myself and had failed. Now the lines of one of my favorite prayers assumed greater significance for me: 'I lay all my affairs in Thy hand. Thou art my Guide and my Refuge.'

In time the guidance came. Gradually, I began to rely more and more on the Bahá'í Writings to fight my battle. For me, guidance came after pondering such verses as the following statement of Bahá'u'lláh:

> O contending peoples and kindreds of the earth! Set your faces towards unity, and let the radiance of its light shine upon you. Gather ye together, and for the sake of God resolve to root out whatever is the source of contention amongst you.

I realized that my purpose in overcoming my racism was more than to rid myself of guilt and shame. I was to do it 'for the sake of God'. Overcoming my personal racism for any other reason, I learned later, would indicate how much I really loved God. With that understanding, my focus shifted in dealing with my problem. Whatever effort I made to overcome racism, whether it be personal or community-wide, I viewed as an expression of my love for God. I did it because I knew that that's what He desired, and I wanted to please Him.

With that perspective the ache in my heart eventually disappeared. There would be no more self-flagellation, no more wallowing in self-pity. My personal battle took on a broader thrust, becoming more positive. A new vision dominated my thinking.

I realized that merely overcoming racism wasn't enough. Once vanquished, what then? In time a new racism would replace the old. The flower must spring from where the weeds once grew. That flower is the human family, united at last as it is meant to be – black, white, red, yellow, all shades of flesh, reaching as one to the Sun of their creation – reaching for life.

I knew then, without any doubt, what I had to do. I had to comply with God's law that all people, regardless of color, must live in harmony. It became evident that the more I loved God, the more I wanted to adhere to His laws. Whenever I pondered the following verse from Bahá'u'lláh's Writings I wanted to embrace all humans, regardless of their color. My heart swelled with love:

O Children of Men!
Know ye not why We created you all from the same dust? That no one should exalt himself over the other. Ponder at all times in your hearts how ye were created. Since We have created you all from one same substance it is incumbent on you to be even as one soul, to walk with the same feet, eat with the same mouth and dwell in the same land, that from your inmost being, by your deeds and actions, the signs of oneness and the essence of detachment may be made manifest. Such is My counsel to you, O concourse of light! Heed ye this counsel that ye may obtain the fruit of holiness from the tree of wondrous glory.

It became obvious that I could not solve my problem by dwelling on it; I wasn't capable of solving it. In the past I had tried and become frustrated and angry, and worse than that, spiritually immobilized. Not dwelling on it, however, didn't mean I shouldn't be aware of my problem. I had to be – just as a recovering alcoholic is aware of what one drink could do to him. Dwelling on his problem, however, would eventually weaken his resolve to stay sober. But by focusing his thoughts on God and drawing strength from Him he's able to transcend the impulse to drink and find new direction and hope.

Yes, overcoming racism is like overcoming alcoholism! What's most important is acknowledging your disease. Seeking and getting the right help is essential, and following the prescription is necessary. Generally, the recovering alcoholic who subscribes to the guidelines of Alcoholics Anonymous doesn't fall back. He is able to repulse all enticements, resist all temptations. And part of his treatment is active involvement in helping others suffering from the same affliction to stay sober.

I found the teachings of my Faith essential to solving my problem:

> Let the white make a supreme effort in their resolve to contribute their share to the solution of this problem, to abandon once for all their usually inherent and at times subconscious sense of superiority, to correct their tendency towards revealing a patronizing attitude towards the members of the other race, to persuade them through their intimate, spontaneous and informal association with them of the genuineness of their friendship and the sincerity of their intentions, and to master their impatience of any lack of responsiveness on the part of a people who have received, for so long a period, such grievous and slow-healing wounds. Let the negroes, through a corresponding effort on their part, show by every means in their power the warmth of their response, their readiness to forget the past, and their ability to wipe out every trace of suspicion that may still linger in their hearts and minds.

'Abdu'l-Bahá, the son of Bahá'u'lláh, inspired me through the example of his life. Learning how he dealt with racism when he visited North America in 1912 provided me with more positive direction.

'Abdu'l-Bahá referred to racism as a 'wound' and a 'disease'. Yet in his travels throughout America he didn't rail against racism. Instead, he tried to draw Blacks and whites together. He addressed the importance of racial unity whenever the opportunity arose, both in large gatherings like the 1912 NAACP convention, or in dealings with individuals in their homes or on the street. His happiest moments in America were spent in meetings where Blacks and whites mingled freely. Time and again he overturned the prevailing American view that whites were inherently superior to Blacks.

In 'Abdu'l-Bahá I found a model of how to work for racial unity.

While 'Abdu'l-Bahá took bold action when it was required, it was never offensive. His approach was never condescending; it was more like a friend sharing news of an impending danger and offering guidance on how to avoid it. His contribution wasn't confined to words. In fact, what made the greatest impression on me was what he did.

'Abdu'l-Bahá saw beauty in blackness. Through his deeds he shared what he knew, and those who witnessed them learned great lessons. Howard Colby Ives, a Christian minister then, was such a witness.

A group of New York boys, around 13 and 14 years old, who wanted to meet 'Abdu'l-Bahá got their wish. Among them was a black youngster, who seemed to tag along. Mr Ives never forgot that visit:

> When his visitors had arrived, 'Abdu'l-Bahá had sent out for some candy and now it appeared, a great five-pound box of expensive mixed chocolates. It was unwrapped and 'Abdu'l-Bahá walked with it around the circle of boys, dipping His hand into the box and placing a large handful in the hands of each, with a word and smile for everyone. He then returned to the table at which He had been sitting, and laying down the box, which now had only a few pieces in it, He picked from it a long chocolate nougat; it was very black. He looked at it a moment and then around at the group of boys who were watching Him intently and expectantly. Without a word, He walked across the room to where the colored boy was sitting, and, still without speaking, but with a humorously piercing glance that swept the group, laid the chocolate against the black cheek. His face was radiant as He laid His arm around the shoulder of the boy and that radiance seemed to fill the room. No words were necessary to convey His meaning, and there could be no doubt that all the boys caught it.
>
> You see, He seemed to say, that he is not only a black flower, but also a black sweet. You eat black chocolates and find them good; perhaps you would find this black brother of yours good also if you taste his sweetness.
>
> Again that awed hush fell over the room. Again the boys all looked with real wonder at the colored boy as if they had never

seen him before, which indeed was true. And as for the boy himself, upon whom all eyes were now fixed, he seemed perfectly unconscious of all but 'Abdu'l-Bahá. Upon Him his eyes were fastened with an adoring, blissful look such as I had never seen upon any face. For the moment he was transformed. The reality of his being had been brought to the surface and the angel he really was revealed.

'Abdu'l-Bahá was aware of America's racial segregation policies. Even in the nation's capital no fraternization between Blacks and whites was condoned. While in Washington DC 'Abdu'l-Bahá defied the segregation custom at a reception that was given in his honor. Explorer Admiral Peary, inventor Alexander Graham Bell, and the Turkish ambassador were among the guests, along with a number of prominent politicians and socialites. An hour before the luncheon 'Abdu'l-Bahá met with Louis Gregory, a young black man and lawyer, who had become a Bahá'í in 1909.

When luncheon was announced, Mr Gregory slipped away because it wasn't acceptable for Blacks to dine with whites, especially in such distinguished company. Concerned, 'Abdu'l-Bahá asked his host to find the young lawyer. A few minutes later, Mr Gregory, the son of a slave, was escorted into the elegant dining room by the host. Harlan Ober, a luncheon guest, recalled the rest:

> 'Abdu'l-Bahá, Who was really the Host (as He was wherever He was), had by this time rearranged the place setting and made room for Mr Gregory, giving him the seat of honor at His right. He stated He was very pleased to have Mr Gregory there, and then, in the most natural way as if nothing unusual had happened, proceeded to give a talk on the oneness of mankind.

Interestingly, not a single white person at the table objected to 'Abdu'l-Bahá's radical action.

When in New York, 'Abdu'l-Bahá was impressed by the way the white Bahá'ís responded to an act of racial discrimination leveled against their fellow black Bahá'ís.

A hotel proprietor refused to allow any Blacks into his hotel, where the Bahá'ís had planned a meeting. He claimed that if the people saw that one colored person had entered the hotel, no respectable person would ever set foot in it and his business would go to the wind.

The next day a special banquet was held for the black believers in the home of a Bahá'í. The whites insisted on serving their black brothers and sisters. After witnessing this act of love, 'Abdu'l-Bahá said, 'Behold the influence and the effect of the words of Bahá'u'lláh, that have removed hatred and strangeness, erased these prejudices, made you serve one another with sincerity.'

In a wholly unprecedented move, 'Abdu'l-Bahá instigated, encouraged and witnessed the marriage of Louis Gregory and Louisa Mathew, a white Englishwoman. That single act has inspired many Bahá'ís the world over to seek a mate of different color.

Before leaving America, 'Abdu'l-Bahá declared that eliminating racism and establishing racial unity was not only essential to the health of the nation but would have an even greater benefit: '. . . the accomplishment of unity between the colored and whites will be an assurance of the world's peace.'

But while 'Abdu'l-Bahá promoted the establishment of planetary racial harmony, he also warned what would happen if the races remained divided in America:

> When I was in America, I told the white and colored people that it was incumbent upon them to be united or else there would be the shedding of blood. I did not say more than this so that they might not be saddened. But, indeed, there is a greater danger than only the shedding of blood. It is the destruction of America.

18

FINALLY, I understood that all of the berating of myself that I had engaged in while trying to solve my problem had been destructive. It not only immobilized me spiritually, it made me more self-centered, drawing me further away from what I should have been doing: becoming a force for racial unity wherever I happened to be.

Fortified by prayer, inspired by 'Abdu'l-Bahá's example, armed with guidelines of the Bahá'í teachings, and with a sincere desire to succeed, I embarked, at the age of 55, on a lifelong commitment to work for racial unity. I went ahead, believing that my pursuing this goal would make all things right. I wasn't going to waste another minute worrying about my problem. Instead, I was going to direct my energies into building bridges between whites and people of color.

I wasn't naive. I knew that I wasn't going to perform miracles, uniting thousands, or even hundreds, of people – although should something like that happen I wasn't going to reject it! The chances of something like that happening, however, were extremely slim. In fact, I tried to push that kind of thought out of my mind. To be effective, I had to be realistic. My primary responsibility, I realized, was to try to demonstrate by example the principle of the oneness of humankind in the neighborhood where I lived, where I worked and where I played. It meant creating a home where all people would feel truly loved. It meant being involved in combatting racism in the schools, if possible, by helping to weave the principle of the oneness of humankind into all subjects taught. It meant helping to create a healthy interracial climate in my community: holding regular meetings in my home where the oneness of humankind is discussed and the real history of America's Blacks is revealed. It meant developing in my workplace a harmonious interracial atmosphere, where everyone, regardless of color or ethnic origin, feels comfortable with everyone else. Actually, it came down to being a force for racial unity at all times.

Success, I realized, was not going to be determined by how many people I helped to unite. In the long run, success will be measured by how pure my motives are, how well I follow the example of 'Abdu'l-Bahá and the Bahá'í guidelines, and above all, how consistent I am in drawing strength and direction from God. Following that regimen will produce the right results.

I also knew that success wouldn't come about by sitting around wishing for improvement in America's racial climate. Even praying and doing nothing, when physically capable of taking action, won't really help. As a Bahá'í I knew that faith is seen as 'conscious knowledge acted upon'. In other words, to be faithful, I had to carry out what I knew was right. Louis Gregory certainly understood that.

Louis Gregory dedicated his life to working to unify the human family. As a Bahá'í he had to do it because it was a basic spiritual principle. Besides being a prolific writer and speaker on the topic, he actively worked to bring together people who traditionally were socially separated. His campaigns in the deep South even concerned some Bahá'ís. They were afraid that he would end up hanging from some tree in Mississippi or Alabama. While he appreciated their concern, he went ahead with his unity excursions, often with a white man from the North – this to dramatize the principle of the oneness of humankind. Often black as well as white communities drove him out of town, because they didn't want anyone upsetting the status quo. But there were some people, Blacks and whites, who embraced his ideas and internalized them, becoming spiritual powerhouses, unafraid to express their true feelings and live out their beliefs in a dangerous situation.

What Louis Gregory did in the early 1920s had a lasting effect, though most of the people at the time had little appreciation of his sacrifices. In many ways his efforts set the stage for racial integration in the South. While most communities remained segregated, black and white Bahá'ís met regularly and worked together to foster better human relations.

Because they were small in number and pacific in nature, the Bahá'í groups didn't arouse much attention. Nevertheless, there were those in the community at large who weren't blind to what the Bahá'ís were doing. In fact, in the mid-1950s a University of North Carolina Dean approached Carolyn Wooten, a Bahá'í who was one of the secretaries at the school, and told her, 'I would like to see our university racially integrated. The reason I mention this to you is because I've been watching the Bahá'ís over the years and have been impressed with the racial harmony you people practice.

'Because of your example,' he went on to say, 'I would like to see the Bahá'ís hold a conference at our university so that the faculty, administrators and students could see that Blacks and whites can get along together as equals.'

Shortly after the Bahá'í conference, the University of North Carolina admitted its first black students.

There were other Bahá'ís who followed the path that Louis Gregory blazed. Roy Williams, for example, traveled around the country, holding racial amity meetings. In 1921 he organized a conference in Springfield, Massachusetts, where 1,200 Blacks and whites gathered for the first time on a social basis. So unusual was this that it was headlined on the front page of the local newspaper.

Through the years many others contributed meaningfully to the cause of racial unity, often in an inconspicuous fashion. Eventually, the continual public pronouncements, the regular unity meetings, the natural racial mixing in homes helped to create in many communities a social oasis where many people found refuge and an opportunity to develop their new awareness of the oneness of humankind.

While there were several thousand Bahá'í communities in America in the 1980s, they were small groups, lacking the glitter needed to attract the attention of the masses who had grown accustomed to being wooed by extravagant and spectacular events. Another reason why the great majority of Blacks and whites didn't notice what the Bahá'ís were doing was society's mounting social and economic problems. Fear of change was still another reason. On the other hand, the Bahá'ís have to share the blame. We have been too timid in our efforts to explain to the rest of the population our views on racial unity.

I grew more audacious after studying the 1983 message from the supreme governing body of the Bahá'ís, the Universal House of Justice. It urged all Bahá'ís to become engaged in economic and social development wherever they lived. The idea was to apply Bahá'í solutions to existing economic and social problems. The Bahá'í motive, the message emphasized, was to help improve people's material and social situation.

Believing that the number one social problem in the United States was racism, I decided to make my commitment to its eradication my social and economic development project.

It was easier to do something concrete at work (I was now teaching at a community college) than in the town where I lived. As a college teacher I had some authority; I could set the tone in the classroom and share with my students information that could broaden their understanding of racism in America. Through my efforts I could create a spirit of familyhood among the students – black, white and Hispanic.

I wove into my television communications lessons a human development element that stressed the principle of the oneness of humankind.

So far it has worked well. Usually the first few months of the class the black and white students are polarized, as they are on the outside. The Blacks are clustered together, and there is little interaction between the two groups. By the end of the first semester, however, genuine friendships are developing between them. At graduation they are often close as cousins.

There have been many positive results, but the experience I will best remember occurred at a commencement exercise a few years ago before 8,000 people at the Springfield Civic Center. One of my former students who was studying communications law at the University of Michigan had been asked to be one of the graduation speakers.

When he rose to speak, I felt like a proud father. Tears came to my eyes as he spoke.

'The most important thing', he said, 'that I learned in college was to love and respect my fellow human beings; and I learned that here.

'Look to your left and right, at the people sitting next to you. They are your cousins, for everyone on our tiny planet is related to one another; that means us, every single one of us in this giant arena! We are related to each other, regardless of skin color or surname. Everyone on earth is at least a 50th cousin.'

He then asked everybody to grasp the hands of the people sitting next to them and not let go until he had finished speaking. Everyone I could see obeyed his request.

Everyone was moved by what he said. The keynote speaker, an MIT Vice President, commented during his turn at the podium, 'How can I top what has just been stated? The young man touched on a reality that is a lot more important than a college degree, good grades and an outstanding job.'

Though there have been high moments in carrying out my commitment, there have been some low moments as well, mistakes made by trying too hard. I remember one mistake in particular. Painful at first, the incident forced me to take stock of my approach to all people, but especially Blacks. Sometimes my direct manner is construed as domineering, a quality usually associated with a sense of superiority. Others like Ken see it as patronizing.

When I learned that Ken was looking for work, I offered to help him. Since he had some journalism experience, I contacted a local TV news director on Ken's behalf. It turned out the news director, who was a friend of mine, was looking for a black TV reporter. A large segment of his station's market was black, and a black face on the TV screen, he felt, could help boost the ratings of his major newscast.

Though Ken was hired, he kept looking for another job, one with more responsibility and more pay. After all, he reasoned, with a Master's degree in journalism he deserved something better than a simple reporter's job.

His attitude bothered me. He should be more appreciative of what I had done for him, I thought. I had put my credibility on the line in supporting his candidacy for the job. If he didn't work out, I feared the next person I recommended wouldn't be seriously considered.

I urged Ken to be more conscientious, though I wasn't sure he wasn't doing his best. I tried to explain how his present job could lead to a newscaster's position, which would pay much more.

It seems that after my series of talks with Ken he intensified his job search. He wanted to be a producer. Yet prior to his present position he had spent a year trying to find work without success.

Ken was a natural reporter. He wrote well and asked intelligent questions. I really felt he would succeed further professionally as a reporter than a producer. But Ken had a different view of himself. Unfortunately, I didn't take that into consideration. Non-verbally, I was telling Ken that I knew what was best for him. My continuous checking to see how he was doing only aggravated the situation. I noticed that the more I got involved in his career, the more he avoided me. I felt bad, because my desire to help him was genuine. I liked the guy and I wanted him to succeed, especially since he was black.

When I began to wonder why he was so ungrateful for what I had done for him, I sensed that perhaps my racism was surfacing. Fortunately, I didn't panic. I dropped out of Ken's life for awhile and tried to assess why our relationship had soured.

135

After reflecting on the situation, it became clear that I had been smothering him like an overbearing mother. He was no child; in fact, we were practically the same age. Had I treated him like a fellow adult – an equal – I would have arranged for the news director to meet him and offered to consult with Ken only when he wished it, and left it at that. The saving grace was that I knew the nature of my mistake and what I had to do to curb my tendency to patronize people like Ken.

Though Ken's contract wasn't renewed, he found a job more to his liking, producing a noon newscast for a TV station in a much larger city. When I learned of his new position, I called Ken to congratulate him and made no reference to his previous job. In time, our relationship improved.

19

IN CARRYING out my commitment I have had to face some tough facts, facts that are difficult to accept in light of the sacrifices made through the years by Blacks and whites who have tried to establish racial equality in America.

Because there is little genuine social interaction between Blacks and whites today, it is extremely difficult to draw the races together. Generally, whites don't want to do it, and Blacks are convinced that it is impossible to do: they are no longer willing to waste their time and energy in efforts that have repeatedly produced frustration and disappointment. Consequently, much black energy is channeled into improving their personal lot through whatever means possible and adopting a 'take care of our own' attitude. This new attitude in the black community has hardened, creating a condition that most whites secretly applaud, because it keeps Blacks out of their neighborhoods, schools and social clubs and has resurrected the 'separate but equal' social pattern that was always separate but never equal during the sixty years it was in operation.

While it upsets me, I can understand why today's Blacks are reluctant to become involved in another struggle for total integration. Time and again they have been rejected or misled. When the black man tried to vote, he was turned away; when he tried to live in a white neighborhood, he was chased back to the ghetto; when he volunteered to protect his country's freedoms during two world wars, he was denied the right to fight and die alongside his white countrymen. Even during the civil rights revolution his open-armed rush into the white man's world was repulsed. Consequently, the distrust of whites among Blacks is so deeply rooted that even genuine white offers of reconciliation are now spurned.

Also – and this is very important – the concept of integration as proposed by this society is not necessarily viewed as a positive idea by many Blacks today. To them integration now means being welcomed into the white man's world and allowed to adapt to values and standards created by whites. In other words, Blacks are given the right to become white-like; they are given the freedom to pursue the American dream, which was never meant for Blacks to realize.

Most people of color don't want to pay that kind of price. They don't want to give up those aspects of their culture which have been a source of joy and strength to them.

Deep down they seek unity with their white brothers and sisters, a unity based on understanding and appreciation of different cultural characteristics, an opportunity to work together as equals in creating a new, more realistic set of values and social standards that is based on justice, not on the misguided notion that the white Anglo-Saxon Protestant way of life is the ideal – a concept the Founding Fathers fostered and everyone else, including immigrants, has tried hard to follow for the past 200 years.

Considering the prevailing polarized racial condition, most current social observers have concluded that absolute integration is far from being realized and may never materialize. That observation, I believe, is related to the fact that not much progress has been made in executing the 'revolutionary change' in the whites' concept and attitude towards Blacks that the Bahá'í Faith called for more than 50 years ago.

As I surveyed the American racial situation in early 1987 I couldn't help but recall what 'Abdu'l-Bahá had warned would happen if the races remained divided. I became convinced that a bloody, nationwide clash between Blacks and whites was inevitable, due mainly to the deteriorating social and economic condition of the majority of Blacks. They have been evolving into an under-class, and there has been no significant means of reversing the slide.

The government has been contributing to the tragedy by fostering a benign policy of neglect, making many Blacks dependent on the welfare system. This has broken their spirit, has robbed them of their dignity, and led some into a life of crime and violence. Birth-out-of-wedlock has been on the rise among Blacks, as has dependency on drugs and alcohol. The highest percentage of unemployed has been among young Blacks, while most of their elders are terribly under-employed. And education, which was supposed to improve their economic condition, hasn't helped of late, for more and more young black men and women have been opting out of college. Those who do go to college often quit before earning a degree. And while all of this has been going on, many of those Blacks who managed to reach middle class status have refused to recognize the growth of the under-class for fear it will reflect poorly on themselves, creating in them a sense of guilt and shame. The worsening living conditions and growing resentment of the black community has been moving steadily towards the explosion point. It seems that blood will run through the streets of America, human blood, flowing from the wounds of both Blacks and whites and sadly mixing in death.

God knows I didn't want to come to that conclusion. I am an optimist at heart, but the evidence was overwhelming. And I began to doubt the merit of my commitment. Seeing the magnitude of America's problem, my efforts seemed inconsequential. I felt like a gnat struggling to fly like an eagle. Yet there were times, especially after prayer, when I would become more hopeful. But that feeling was difficult to sustain all of the time; and reading the newspaper and watching television news didn't help.

In meditating on the problem, I realized I could do something: I could pray more.

No special place is required for prayer. I could pray at work as well as at home. No book is required. I could pray in my classroom and office, for prayer is communication with God. In a second I could share with God a silent appeal and just as quickly feel a surge of energy and become refocused. In that state of mind I seemed to don a special armor that shielded me from the pessimism that the apparent hopelessness of the black–white condition can easily generate in us.

But the effects of prayer aren't everlasting – at least not for me. I didn't always remember to pray; and when I forgot I would swing into a more negative mood or revert to my natural inclination to devise quick and grandiose ways of solving complex problems like racism.

Part of me was still driven by a desire to be involved in a grand race unity project, to be seen to be making significant strides in unifying large numbers of people and improving their social and economic conditions. I wanted to feel the rush of hope that I believed would come from actively participating in such a scheme. I wanted to be part of the building of a world order where race prejudice would no longer be a barrier keeping the human family from realizing its destiny – the coming together in love. Nothing would bring me greater happiness than that.

But I wasn't involved in such a project, and there were no prospects of participating in one. I began to wonder whether the Bahá'ís were too small a force to make a difference.

But that other part of me – the spiritual me, that over the years I have grown to depend on more and more – knew I couldn't give up my commitment. To do so would counteract an important spiritual responsibility. Whenever I would falter in my conviction I would think of 'Abdu'l-Bahá. I tried to pray harder for the strength and courage that was needed to beat back the influences of a skeptical world.

I finally realized that I couldn't control the actions of a community or the thinking of others. In fact, I had no right to do that. All I could do was to make sure that I did what was spiritually responsible. I had to push ahead, doing what I was doing with greater intensity. If I carried on, then the right opportunities to serve in a unifying capacity would come my way.

While watching television one Sunday evening in mid-February 1987, I received a desperate phone call from Alethia King, a Bahá'í student at Smith College and the mother of two young daughters. Her cousin, Juree Harland, who came up from Atlanta to help take care of Alethia's children, had been the target of racist attacks at the Northampton High School where she was taking her last semester.

The word 'nigger' had been painted on her locker room door. One anti-Black note she received read, 'Go back where you came from; we don't like jungle bunnies in Northampton.' Another student called her a 'spear-chucker'. While crossing the street one day a group of students tried to run her down with their car. Juree was in a state of shock. Her cousin's appeal to the principal was met by a denial that there was racism in the school. He claimed that what had happened to Juree had been isolated incidents.

My wife and I decided to contact Phyllis Gudger-Porter, a black Bahá'í who had had considerable experience as a civil rights worker in the '60s. Alethia had called her too.

We arranged a meeting of Bahá'ís and asked Alethia and Juree to explain what had happened at the school. At that gathering, we assured Alethia and Juree of our continuous support and pledged to investigate the situation.

A group called the Pioneer Valley Force for Racial Unity was formed at our second meeting. Its purpose was to combat racism in the Valley, but more important, to work at drawing the races together.

We felt it essential to have men and women who weren't Bahá'ís in the organization. Ours was not a religious crusade. We simply wanted to provide an opportunity for all people of goodwill to work at overcoming America's most serious social problem. We also knew that a variety of viewpoints would enrich our consultations, making for wiser decisions. Men and women of other Faiths, as well as non-church-goers, became active members, contributing meaningfully to policy decisions and participating in the day-to-day operation.

The first thing we did was to write letters to both the principal and the Superintendent of Schools, calling for an investigation into the incidents and for steps to be taken to prevent further racist attacks. The letters were hand-delivered by a special delegation. Sadly, the meetings were non-productive. In fact, the principal said nothing to our group, not even offering them a seat.

To ascertain the true social climate at the high school, we arranged to meet with as many minority students as possible. Nine showed up, including two parents. What we learned from them was heart-wrenching. At first the students were hesitant to share their true feelings for fear of getting into trouble with their teachers and the school administrators and being singled out as trouble-makers by their classmates.

An hour after they arrived they opened up. One young man, who had always wanted to be an electrical engineer, said he had given up the idea after moving to Northampton. Though an 'A' student in Cleveland, his grades fell sharply shortly after transferring. He was forced to switch to a less rigorous academic program. Other young men and women told similar stories. They felt uncomfortable at the school. To fit in they had to do things that felt unnatural. There were no real black or Hispanic role models, and there was little or no reference to their cultures in what they studied. In many ways they felt like foreigners but worse, because most foreign students received special treatment from their teachers and students, and they weren't subjected to racist attacks. No matter what the Blacks and Hispanics did they always felt like outsiders, and they desperately wanted to fit in.

After that meeting we believed that what had happened to Juree resulted from a racist atmosphere that pervaded the school. While it was important to guarantee Juree's safety, we had a much greater challenge – eliminating racism from Northampton High School. It seemed an impossible task. We didn't have the funds or legal expertise to take on a city school system that had a progressive reputation and a lot of money behind it. All our small group had was a sincere desire to correct a bad situation.

We wrote to the mayor, hoping he would help. His response was vague and non-committal.

While wondering what major thing to do next, we did little organizational tasks. We published a pamphlet, explaining the mission of the Pioneer Valley Force for Racial Unity, and we rented a post office box.

We were heartened when Albert Humphries became an active member of our group. He was one of the parents who had attended the fact-finding meeting we had had with the minority students. It turned out that Albert knew the US Justice Department agent who was in the area working on a big racism case at the University of Massachusetts. The agent, Ed McClure, took an immediate interest in our project and started attending our strategy-mapping meetings on his own. Fortunately, Ed had a wealth of experience in combatting racial discrimination in schools. His commonsense approach to his work, he said, was developed in the tough black Brooklyn neighborhood where he had grown up.

Ed's advice to us was to press the school system, even the city, to establish a civil rights policy. Without one the school system wasn't legally accountable for most acts of discrimination within its jurisdiction.

Our determination to carry on with our struggle was due, in large measure, to the continual encouragement Ed gave us, in person and through countless phone calls. One of our important victories was persuading Ed's boss to assign him to our project.

Another victory was securing the help of the Springfield branch of the National Association for the Advancement of Colored People. Its President, Ida Flynn, assigned its chief counsel, Arthur Serota, to our case. His services didn't cost us a penny. Arthur was a fierce human rights advocate; politicians in the region shuddered at the prospect of tangling with him. Of course, we weren't looking for a fight. In fact, we didn't want to take an adversarial approach to the problem, or be divisive in any way.

143

Our interest was to help the principal and the Superintendent of Schools solve the racism problem at the high school. We had the human resources to do that. The last thing we wanted was a legal battle.

In Arthur's letter to the Superintendent of Schools, he outlined what we perceived to be the problem and listed the steps which, we felt, would go a long way to solving it.

We felt there had to be an on-going program to sensitize teachers, administrators and students on how to detect racism and overcome it; that the concept of the oneness of humankind should be woven into the school's curriculum, and that the black and Hispanic contributions to America's development as a nation also be included; that black and Hispanic teachers, counselors and administrators should be hired. We also offered our services in setting up the anti-racism educational program. Finally, the Superintendent of Schools was given more than a month to review our proposals. Failure to comply, or even to show a sincere interest in the possible implementation of our recommendations, Arthur warned, would force us to file a complaint with the Massachusetts Commission against Discrimination. April 20th was the deadline.

There was a quick response to the letter. The school system's Boston-based lawyer asked for a meeting three weeks before the deadline.

I was ecstatic. We were finally being heard. Though a lot had to be done before we could celebrate, I felt optimistic that some good would result from our efforts. We had been meeting once or twice a week for more than six weeks – writing letters, making phone calls, mailing pamphlets to people who expressed interest in what the Pioneer Valley Force for Racial Unity was doing. And there were the daily calls to Juree to boost her morale. As a show of support for Alethia and Juree we held our meetings in their apartment.

Going to school every day was difficult for Juree, for false word had spread that she was involved in a campaign to embarrass the school. Students shunned her and some teachers saw her as a loud-mouthed trouble-maker from the South. What hurt Juree the most was that a few black students became angry with her, accusing her of upsetting their efforts to fit into the predominantly white school. But Juree persevered, helped largely by the continuous support she received from her cousin.

April 7th, the day we met with the school system's lawyers, was unusually mild. Inside the high school conference room, however, I sensed a storm brewing. Sitting on the far side of the long rectangular table were two lawyers from one of the most prestigious law firms in New England. Behind them were the Superintendent of Schools, the high school principal and the vice principal. Not far away was the outgoing Associate Superintendent of Schools who was responsible for hiring minority teachers and staff.

Arthur Serota, Ed McClure, Alethia King, Ida Flynn, Peter Vaughn, Phyllis Gudger-Porter and I were on the other side of the table.

The lawyers declared that their investigation had shown that our charge of racism at the high school was baseless, that what had happened to Juree was an isolated case. They proposed establishing a mechanism in the school that would address further racist acts. We, on the other hand, argued that racist acts don't materialize out of thin air; they are the by-product of a racist atmosphere and that atmosphere must be cleaned up. Our attempt to explain what racism is, and how it is manifested, made no impression on the lawyers who did all of the talking for the school system. The three male administrators remained tight-lipped throughout the proceedings. When Ida Flynn asked why there were no black teachers at the high school, the administrator in charge of minority recruitment said, 'We can't find any candidates around here.'

'Did you ever consider recruiting outside of western Massachusetts?' Mrs Flynn asked.

'No.'

'I'm sure you'll find good prospects at Howard and Fisk, or at some schools in New York.'

It seemed that hiring black faculty members had a low priority in Northampton, perhaps because the school administrators felt there was no need for black teachers. Racism, they believed, didn't exist in their schools.

After the meeting we chatted with the school administrators and found them all to be fine people, although we learned later that the principal had complained to someone that it was the Bahá'ís who were causing all of the trouble.

God knows we weren't trying to be mischievous. On the contrary, we wanted to be helpful. The problem was that the administrators couldn't recognize the disease that was psychologically crippling the human beings they were charged with educating.

Evidently the lawyers thought we were bluffing about complaining to the Commission against Discrimination, because on April 20th there was no response from them. We filed the complaint and held a news conference. Yes, a news conference! We had withheld the story from the news media for nearly three months. Now the Pioneer Valley Force for Racial Unity felt it was time to apply pressure: trying to reason with the school system hadn't worked. That night the story was on television news. The following morning it was headlined in the daily newspapers. All day long we received phone calls from men and women who expressed sympathy for our cause. Some of them had children in the school system and asked if they could work with us. We welcomed their help.

I was thrilled. All our work was paying off. What had started as a stab in the dark by a seemingly powerless little group of concerned people was gaining focus, a sharper view of how to achieve its goal.

Many city residents were stunned by our charges; others were defensive, saying, 'This sort of thing can't happen in a place like Northampton. It can't be true, for ours is a socially progressive city – it always has been.'

Teachers and students at the high school were reacting nervously about the charges. Rumors abounded. Day after day there were new stories in the city's newspaper. Some teachers feared that they were going to be replaced by Blacks and Hispanics. With some, the controversy pushed their prejudice to the surface.

We held a special meeting for the Northampton residents who had volunteered to help us. Alethia's dining room was packed with people who were outraged by the revelations of the high school's true social condition and the way its administrators were handling the Juree Harland case. Two newspaper reporters were on hand.

After sharing with the newcomers our organization's purpose and plans, we consulted on what we could do together to help the cause.

We agreed to draft a petition calling for improvement in race relations at the high school. The petition was drafted that evening, and almost everyone volunteered to circulate it throughout the city. After gathering about a thousand signatures, it would be presented to the mayor. We also organized a ribbon-wearing campaign. A woman offered to prepare the black and white ribbons; others volunteered to distribute them. Those who wore them would be proclaiming their support for Juree and our cause. Finally, we all felt it would be best if a separate group was formed, composed only of Northampton residents, that could join with the Force for Racial Unity in pressing for the changes we had recommended to the school system. The consensus was that a school system would react more favorably to its town's taxpayers than to a group made up mainly of outsiders. Contact with the new group – the Committee for Multi-Racial Unity – would be maintained primarily by the Force members residing in Northampton. The next day the newspapers carried stories about our meeting.

While we were impressed with the continuous news coverage, what impressed us even more was the editorial that appeared in the leading daily newspaper:

It is always easier for white people to explain away racial attacks as

147

isolated incidents. However, any act born of racial intolerance, no matter how small, is an assault on the individual and should not be tolerated.

As administrators, Northampton school officials might have made stronger and more timely statements decrying these ugly acts. Their responses could have shown more compassion for the student and more sensitivity toward other minorities in the school.

An urgency to act seems lacking. Even the School Committee was not immediately told about the incident and even last week some members were still not fully informed about what happened.

As educators, school officials missed an opportunity to turn the racial incident into a learning experience for the students. The chance to act boldly was available that day in February when Juree Harland walked into the principal's office and told of racial graffiti on her locker door and an insulting note. She was new to the school, having just moved here from Atlanta, and the racial slurs were a shock to her.

From various accounts, it appears school officials treated the attacks as a legal problem, a case to be solved. When Principal Gordon Noseworthy took to the public address system, it was to discount rumors that Juree Harland was a narcotics agent. He never spoke of the racial slurs.

We felt we had to respond through the letter-to-the-editor column, hoping it would catch the eye of the local educators and the city's School Committee:

To the Editor,
Daily Hampshire Gazette:

We wish to commend you for your recent editorial regarding the Juree Harland case at Northampton High School. You were able to see beyond the obvious, recognizing that what happened to Ms Harland in February can't be dismissed as 'just an isolated incident'. The climate that produces such anti-social behavior has to be addressed. For there could be more like incidents in the future, or worse. There have been others in the past.

Unfortunately, we are dealing with something intangible, and that creates a problem. Most people can't recognize it and therefore claim it doesn't exist. Racism is more than segregation and discrimination. It is a social virus; its chief symptom being a sub-conscious feeling of superiority. Often the perpetrators aren't aware of the symptom, but minority persons are, for they have been conditioned to survive in an alien culture and therefore can sense the symptom, creating within them an unhealthy tension.

We and the NAACP, and a representative of the Justice Department, tried in our April 7th meeting with the school system's leadership and lawyers to convey this point to them.

Our intent was to approach the school system with an offer to work together in raising the consciousness of the students, faculty, counselors and administrators. The last thing we wanted was to have to take the legal route.

In fact, we purposely kept it from the press, because we were hoping for unified action with the Northampton school system taking a courageous step in dealing with a problem that many school systems in the nation refuse to tackle. The need for change is approaching the critical stage because of the city's growing minority population.

We still think it isn't too late to forge a cross-cultural curriculum that will eventually improve the social climate in the Northampton schools; in the hiring of minority teachers and counselors; in organizing classroom seminars on race relations, as well as parent/ teacher workshops.

We believe that most of the city of Northampton would welcome such an achievement.

THE PIONEER VALLEY FORCE FOR RACIAL UNITY

As the favorable news coverage mounted, we gained consider-able grassroots support from Blacks and whites, many of whom came to our public meetings. When the District Attorney and his wife joined our organization, we knew we were moving closer to achieving our goal.

Momentum gathered when a junior administrator resigned because of an elementary school principal's racist views. Our campaign, we learned later, gave the former nun the courage to act. Her resignation was announced in the newspapers. North-ampton's population was beginning to understand that racism was probably not confined to the high school.

A few days later we read in the newspaper that the school system had arranged for a human relations organization to begin holding sensitivity training sessions for high school students and teachers, hoping it would lead to better race relations.

While we viewed that as a face-saving way of admitting that the charges made by the Force for Racial Unity were accurate, the school system, nevertheless, had taken a step in the right direction and we applauded that. In the meantime, the petition was being circulated throughout the city, and the Northampton Committee for Multi-Racial Unity called on the high school principal with a set of recommendations. Unlike his reaction to our first delegation, he listened intently and promised to put into practice most of the group's requests.

Outside pressure on the school system mounted: the State Department of Education announced that it was going to investigate our charges.

About a week later, at a public civil rights conference staged by the District Attorney, Northampton's mayor proclaimed that his city was drafting a civil rights policy that would be enforced in every municipal department.

The District Attorney, who had been interested in the issue of racism before the Juree Harland case broke, established a bi-county Civil Rights Advisory Board to promote racial harmony through non-formal educational means. Some of our members were appointed to the Board.

About eleven months after we launched our campaign, the State Department of Education notified the Northampton school system that the charges we had leveled against the system were essentially true. The city was urged to correct the situation. Failure to comply could lead to the cutting off of state funding to the local schools.

With some changes in personnel in high positions, the Northampton school system adopted a new, more progressive attitude and vowed to make its schools more comfortable for minority students. The hiring of black, Hispanic and Asian teachers became a top priority.

Northampton was in the throes of social change. It was forced to take a close look at itself, and it found things – ugly things – it never knew existed. Getting rid of racism is tough, but the city has made a start and is making some headway. It thrilled all of us involved in the struggle to think that our organization had helped the city improve its social condition.

I learned a lot from my involvement with the Pioneer Valley Force for Racial Unity. It altered my view of what it takes to run an effective community action campaign.

We didn't need much money. In fact, we didn't have a budget. When money was needed to rent a hall or print a pamphlet, people reached into their pockets and made contributions. We incurred no debts. I guess when you believe deeply in your cause, and you see something positive resulting from your efforts, you are willing to give, perhaps even more than you can afford.

I also learned that you don't need to be highly organized to get things done, provided you are highly motivated and everyone is united in thought. We had no leadership; each meeting was chaired by a different member. Using the Bahá'í method of consultation helped to limit the discussion to the issues and kept it free of posturing and speech-making. No one dominated the group. All decisions were the result of a vote, most of which were unanimous.

Ed McClure was impressed with the way we consulted and got things done. He was amazed that there was no disunity, not even a hint of it; and that no one was trying to use the group to further his own political ambitions. He said he had never worked with a group that was so free of ego and so service-minded.

Another important thing I learned was that if you are working for a cause that's based on carrying out a law of God, you are going to succeed; if those who are aware of the law uphold it wholeheartedly, then all barriers eventually crumble.

From a personal standpoint, the most important thing I learned was that by channeling my energy into promoting racial unity I stopped dwelling on my problem. Further, I was lifted into such an exalted state of mind that I felt no need to dwell on it. I felt I was partaking of an extraordinary elixir. During the entire Northampton high school campaign I never grew tired or discouraged, nor did I experience 'burnout'. Of course there were times when I wanted to stay home to watch a basketball game on television instead of going to another meeting. At those times I would go to the meeting hoping we would finish early enough for me to see the last half. Five minutes into the meeting I would be enveloped by the spirit there and forget about the game.

I certainly wasn't the only one who benefited from the Northampton experience. Everyone involved – Bahá'í and non-Bahá'í – grew from it.

It was heartwarming to see the attitudes of people change, to see their distrust evaporate, to see caring relationships develop between people who were once suspicious of one another. It made me rethink the conclusion I had arrived at earlier in the year regarding the future of black and white relations. There now seemed a chance that that dreaded conflict could be avoided. What was necessary was that the kind of spirit generated by the Pioneer Valley Force for Racial Unity be spread across the land.

One of our co-workers, a learned black woman and veteran civil rights worker, was moved by that spirit. She confessed to Phyllis Gudger-Porter, 'I never thought I would ever trust white people again until I met the white Bahá'ís. They're different. They have made me believe that there is a chance for the human family to come together – in love.'